ReD HeaT

MAUREEN SUAN-NEO

D E D I C A T I O N

For my mother Kim-Neo
who taught me how to cook

and

my husband, John Arumainayagam
whose invaluable help, encouragement and determination
made this book possible.

A C K N O W L E D G E M E N T S

With special thanks to Jhon Kevern whose stunning photography has
made this book an art in itself; to Jim Moriarty, my publisher who has
given his unstinting help in the production of this book; to Valerie Kevern
of Tables Laid for the use of all crockery and backgrounds and Clare
Marshall who helped Jhon and I during the food photography; to Anselm
Robinson for his advice on worldwide distribution; and finally to Tertia
Goodwin for her contribution to the design and layout of the book.

ISBN 0 9527101 0 2
Reproduction - Swaingrove Repro, UK
Printed through World Print, Hong Kong
Fulham Restaurant photograph - Chris Gascoigne

Whilst every care was taken in the preparation of this book, neither the author nor the publisher can accept any liability for any
consequence arising from the use of the information contained.

Published by John Arumainayagam in conjunction with Compass Publications Ltd,
Marcon House, Castle Acre, King's Lynn, Norfolk PE32 2AG   *© 1995 Maureen Suan-Neo*

CONTENTS

INTRODUCTION

Every great cuisine of the world has a tradition of teaching by demonstration, example and word of mouth. Nowhere is this better illustrated than by the Nonyas, who have a deserved reputation for being great cooks.

The daughter of a Peranakan family was not encouraged to have a career. She was brought up to focus her talents on embroidery and the arts, to keep an ordered household and practise her culinary talents for the enjoyment of her husband, his friends and business associates.

My mother was no exception. She learned her skills from her mother, who had in turn learned from hers and so on.

When it came to my generation, sweeping changes in education and the liberation of women, even in the East, had instilled in us different ideas and expectations from life.

Nevertheless I was not spared kitchen duties, and so I, too, learned in the traditional manner. Fastidious and a perfectionist, my mother taught me the full repertoire of Nonya specialities. Nothing pleased her more than the appreciative delight on our faces as we tucked into family meals whose variety of dishes would have seemed a feast to Western eyes.

Imagine then the reaction a real Nonya feast would provoke. I vividly remember as a child accompanying my parents to wedding parties where a long table, or Tok Panjang, would groan under the vast array of Nonya delights. I would have to wait in impatient expectation as people took it in turns to sit down and eat - guests of honour and the elderly being given priority over little girls.

Today, sadly, these elaborate celebrations are increasingly a thing of the past as modern couples resort to hotel catering. Even so such functions can still provide ten courses or more.

As I grew up in cosmopolitan Singapore where food is a national obsession, I learned to take for granted the quality and diversity so readily available. Enjoying a bewildering variety of foods from stalls of every description costs next to nothing. Competition and specialisation ensured the offerings were of high quality and it is therefore no wonder that everybody has at least one meal a day from a stall.

The multi-national fare available throughout the day means breakfast could just as easily comprise Indian dosais and chutneys as Chinese prawn noodles. Lunch could be bought from a Malay stall serving rice with an assortment of meats, vegetables and condiments cooked in traditional style. You could eat out at every meal for a whole month and never repeat a dish.

With this background you will understand why the most difficult aspect of leaving home and country was adjusting to the food. This rapidly prompted me to hone my cooking to the great delight of my husband John, who has a similar background to my own, having been raised in Penang. Drawing on recipes passed down from my mother and her ancestors, I was able to prepare dishes that I had missed since leaving home. This was not an easy task since, as with so many family recipes, few Nonya specialities had been recorded in recipe books, which is one good reason why I have written this one.

However, my ancestral skills proved so popular I found myself giving dinner parties for friends and business associates, at least twice a week. It was only later that I realised how I had unwittingly followed the Nonya tradition, with one major difference - I was also working! Indeed, though our guests were struck by the qualities and flavours of the meals we served, they were also impressed by the fact that I had conjured up what they thought to be feasts on my return from work.

The secret of course was energy.

Not mine; just the magic of electricity. Speedy food processors and blenders are a wonderful substitute for forced labour with a pestle and mortar. Moreover even traditional Far Eastern food takes time only in the preparation, the actual cooking is rapid, with the prepared ingredients being added in quick succession. That, together with elegant presentation, is what makes it appealing, delicious and healthy, while the rhizomes and spices give the impression of elaborate preparation.

Following consistent success amongst our admiring friends, we decided to expose my family secrets to a wider audience and in 1982 we opened our first restaurant in Fulham. We called it Singapura, the Malay for Singapore,

and served Nonya and Singaporean cuisine.

To our pleasant surprise, it was an immediate hit, with foodies in Fulham and Chelsea becoming regulars and pretty soon we were appealing much further afield. Now my cooking began to evolve, encompassing other cuisines from Southeast Asia and adapting to ingredients available in the west. I was able to create new dishes and meet the trend towards healthy eating of lighter foods with subtle spicing. Our travels and eating experiences also made an important contribution.

As the repertoire expanded so did our public. We have since opened two Singapuras in the City of London, which are packed to capacity on most days.

We have been delighted by the popularity of our Nonya based cuisine which we were not sure would appeal to conservative English tastes. Nothing properly prepared us for the regularity with which many 'city gents' return often for exactly the same dishes on consecutive days, while others venture boldly into new territory, eager to sample the entire gamut of the menu.

On reflection, perhaps I should have expected it. The availability in recent years of all the exotic ingredients with the quality and freshness essential to South East Asian cooking has gone a long way to bringing the cuisine of that region to the West.

Anyone with an interest in cooking should have no difficulty in experimenting with our dishes. I have run special cookery classes at the original Singapura for friends and regular customers who had begged me to show them how to prepare the dishes we served there.

They were surprised, as well as delighted, at the relative ease with which they soon presented delicious and apparently complicated meals to appreciative and admiring friends at successful dinner parties.

Now it is your turn. In sharing my recipes with you I am sharing the glorious flavours which are uniquely Nonya as well as a wonderful tradition of whose continuance you can be a welcome part.

NONYAS AND BABAS

The Straits of Malacca is one of the most strategically placed waterways in the world and trading ships from east and west had plied this narrow stretch of water from the first century when India and China held maritime supremacy. The port of Malacca on the western coast of Malaya gained importance as a trading post and by the 15th Century, became the target for invasions by the Portuguese and Spanish who travelled along the breadth of the Far East in search of spices. The prosperity of the Portuguese naval exploits soon attracted rival interests in the Dutch and in 1602 the Dutch East India Company took a foothold in that part of the world. The Dutch monopoly on the spice trade encouraged the British to seek new territories for spices. They found what they were looking for in India and within the same century established the East India Company which grew to become a superpower both commercially and politically.

Burgeoning trade with China made it imperative for the British East India Company to gain access to the Straits of Malacca and in 1786, under the captainship of Sir Francis Light, paid a handsome tribute to the Malay Rulers for the right to occupy the uninhabited island of Penang which is situated off the northern Coast of west Malaya. Jungle land near the sea was cleared to make way for a new port. Under British occupation a rapid influx of pioneers soon made the new settlement thrive and ousted Malacca from its importance as a naval port.

Discovering Singapore

The British, eager to expand their power and dominance in the Far East, and thwart continuing Dutch and French designs in the area, decided to establish another settlement further down the Straits of Malacca. In 1819 Sir Stamford Raffles discovered Singapore, an island swamp lying at the tip of the Malay archipelago with a deep natural harbour which made it the ideal port for passing ships. However, unlike the Dutch in Malacca who levied heavy tolls and imposed all sorts of commercial restrictions, the British authorities declared Singapore a free port. This made it thrive and merchants from China, Annam, Thailand and Borneo landed on the island with cargoes bound for the west and vice versa.

Making Fortunes

Within a few months the population of the settlement grew from a mere handful of jungle natives and fisherfolk to five thousand. The island of Singapore was swarming with Chinese, Malays and Bugis pioneers eager to make their fortunes under the British flag and the harbour was filled with all manner of seagoing vessels. An increasing number of immigrants flooded into Singapore from south China, mainland Malaya, Tamils from south India, Arabs, Armenians and of course the British, attracted by the prospect of free trade and employment opportunities.

The settlements of Penang, Malacca and Singapore became administratively joined together as Anglo-Dutch relationships improved under the Treaty of London and thus was born the collective term for the Straits Settlements.

The inevitable emergence of a hybrid population procreated by Chinamen and local Malay women was thus begun and termed Straits Chinese to distinguish from the mainland Chinese. Local annals had documented that an exchange of Chinese brides to Malay princes also took place, engineered by the Chinese Emperor in an endeavour to promote goodwill and further trade in Southeast Asia. The Straits Chinese living in a colonial environment were educated at English schools and convents run by Christian missionaries. Their language was a curious Malay patois mixed with Chinese dialect and English words. They were Chinese in spirit but Malay in form. The men continued to dress in Chinese costumes whilst the women kept to their maternal Malay dress. They were however among the first to follow English ways and dress, believing this to be a status symbol.

The term Babas was attributed to the men and

Nonyas to the women. They inherited the Chinese entrepreneurial spirit and diligence and became immensely successful, dominating the social and political scene. Enhanced by their English education, they became wealthy and important members of society.

Good Cooks

The role of womenfolk in the early 19th Century was confined to childbearing, housekeeping, crafts and cooking skills and the wealthy Nonyas took the greatest pride in serving up culinary delights that became legendary. Arranged marriages which were practised at the time made it imperative for the Nonya brides to be good cooks, an important consideration which was taken into account by the matchmakers and the groom's household. Combining chinese ingredients such as soya products, soya sauces, beancurds, fermented pastes, and vegetables with the indigenous herbs and aromatic roots such as lemon grass, chillies, galanggal and turmeric, they created a unique cuisine which today bears their title 'Nonya'. The many auspicious days of the Chinese calendar and weddings and social gatherings were celebrated with lavish feasts laid out on a Tok Panjang (long table) to which guests would be invited to partake in turns with deference given to the men and older generation who enjoy the first sitting.

The half-caste status of the Straits Chinese did not lower their self-esteem. In fact, most of them felt themselves superior to the Malays, who were financially less well off, and to the pure Chinese, especially those who were new arrivals to the Straits Settlements. Their English education, affluence, good looks and territorial knowledge made them proud and chauvinistic.

The following generations of Straits Chinese tended to marry into pure Chinese stock rather than Malay, partly because the Chinese heritage was stronger but partly due to religious reasons. As the Malays embraced Islam and were more or less orthodox, the Straits Chinese kept to ancestral worship, Confucianism and Taoism whilst others succumbed to the missionaries and became Christians. Chinese dominance was more pronounced in Singapore and religious festivals and wedding rites followed Chinese customs. The elaborate ceremonial rites of the Nonya weddings spanned twelve days and are still the subject of much interest although rarely practised by today's newlyweds. The Nonyas and Babas were therefore different from their Chinese ancestors only in language and food although in some respects they were better looking than the pure Chinese, as offsprings of mixed marriages have a tendency to be.

It has become difficult to determine who qualified as Babas and Nonyas as intermarriage has diluted the highly individual behaviour and characteristics of the original Baba stock. Western influences have eroded traditions and customs and the attitudes and values of the modern Nonya is no different from any other ethnic group living in the same community. Education and equal opportunities for the women of today meant that the Nonyas relinquished their role in the kitchen, took careers and gained employment in commerce and industry

Love of Good Food

Preparation of family meals has either been relegated to foreign help or reduced to a simple affair or even bought in from the multitude of cheap but quality food stalls that abound in Southeast Asia. It is fortunate therefore that the recipes and lengthy preparations of the Nonya cuisines have been documented and preserved by recipe books. The southeast Asian love of good food has also perpetuated this cuisine which has not only seen a revival in the last decade but its popularity has also spread to foreign shores. The shrinking of the world through widespread tourism has also made it possible for the people of other nations to experience the unique tastes that once were only available in the homes of the Nonyas and the Babas.

A family meal tends to be a simple affair of two or three meat dishes, including seafood, a soup that forms part of the main course, vegetables and rice. Rice forms the staple part of every meal, even if noodles are served.

As a rule, the cuisines of Thailand, Malaysia and Indonesia use fresh aromatic herbs and rhizomes to add flavour and spice up their dishes, rather than the abundance of powdered spices to be found in Indian cooking. I find that such dishes complement the blandish stirfry and broiled Chinese dishes and at the same time seem to go fairly well with the heavily spiced Indian curries. In short, Indian and Chinese cuisines form two ends of the spectrum whilst geographically and foodwise the southeast Asian dishes, although unique in their flavours, occupy middle ground.

It would make sense to choose a balance between fried and braised and gravy based dishes. This is why quite a few soupy dishes are available in order to wet the rice and clear the palate from the many fried dishes that abound. Another consideration is countering the hot spices with simpler stirfried dishes. Textures and colour equally play an important part in determining the success of the meal.

Choosing dishes for entertaining must take into account several other factors. Depending on the occasion, food should be convenient and practical to serve and eat. It would be most awkward to expect your guests to tuck into chilli crabs in their shells, using their fingers to eat when they have been invited to a formal dinner.

It is of vital importance to find out whether your guests are capable of coping with hot dishes and it would make sense therefore to serve at least one or two milder or non-spicy dishes (so that he would have something to eat at least). Variety in this instance is vital not only to treat your guests to different foods but also for guests who would not eat one or other of the dishes.

As a cook, you should bear in mind the practicalities of choosing some dishes that can be prepared in advance and warmed up quickly on the stove or in the oven. Do not choose too many that are best cooked just before serv-ing otherwise you might find yourself in the kitchen throughout the evening until you sit down to dinner. Obviously this comes with practice, knowing when to slip in and out between seeing to your guests and seeing to the food but the same could be said of a European dinner party.

One final consideration in choosing a menu and the preparation of a meal as practised by a Chinese brought up with the concepts of 'yin' and 'yang' is using ingredients that would create a neutral balance.

In essence, the Chinese concept of nutrition is that every food possesses an energy that is either 'heating' or 'cooling', which influences the body's intrinsic balance. Consuming an excess of 'heaty' foods generates heat which causes eruptions on the skin (spots and pimples), sore throats and ulcers, and exacerbate infections. Postive aspects of 'heating' or warming foods are that they generate energy and strength by stimulating the metabolism. Heaty foods include ginger, red meats, carrots, sesame oil, alcohol and certain fruits such as grapes.

In contrast, cooling foods soothe, cleanse and reduce toxic heat but their negative aspects cause runny noses, colds and weakness. Seafood, most vegetables and fruits are 'cooling' although oranges are considered 'heaty'. The exceptionally heaty effect that eating the tropical fruit durian has on the system is a particularly good example. Unless counterbalanced by eating cooling food (we normally eat mangosteens at the same time) we inevitably suffered from sore-throats and bad breath the following day.

On that note, I would add that serving nonya dishes seldom fails to please and invite praises from your guests. One of my students from my cookery classes actually received a round of applause from her guests. The clean strong tastes and rich aromatic flavours make the dishes seem so complicated and difficult to execute that only the experts can do it but in fact takes only time and a little help from this book to help you understand the basics while the rest is a matter of taste and preference.

CLEAVER

A heavy cleaver enables you to chop meat and poultry on the bone into smaller bite-size pieces. The back of the cleaver is useful for cracking open the tough shell of a coconut. Sharp knives are absolutely essential for chopping and finely slicing meats and vegetables.

COFFEE MILL

You will need this to grind dry seed spices like coriander, fennel, peppercorns, and cumin. Reserve a separate bowl attachment, if one is available, solely for spices or your coffee will take on a spicy flavour.

COLANDERS

These are useful for draining noodles and vegetables and allowing them to dry before stirfrying.

DEEP FAT FRYER

Useful if you deepfry often enough to justify the cost of buying one. It is also fairly safe to use and the lid stops splattering fats as well as controlling greasy steam.

ELECTRIC RICE COOKERS

Almost every modern household in Southeast Asia uses an electric rice cooker to steam their rice. This allows the chef to put the rice on without having to check on it and turn the heat off at the appropriate time. Highly recommended if you cook rice often enough.

LIQUIDISER OR MINI PROCESSOR

Either one or both are essential if you intend to make the spicy Nonya curries which use plenty of fresh aromatic herbs, bulbs and rhizomes which have to be ground to a paste. They replace the antiquated pestle and mortar.

SAUCEPANS

Several good quality heavy-based saucepans in varying sizes are essential. Choose stainless steel for optimum wear and Teflon for non-stick qualities, especially for reheating. Enamelled cast iron saucepans like Le Creuset are best for cooking dishes that contain acidics such as lemon juice, lemon grass, tamarind and vinegar. The chemical reaction with the metals causes discoloration and an unhealthy greyish hue can spoil what should have been a brightly coloured turmeric orange curry.

WIRE MESH BASKETS

These small baskets with handles are custom made to allow you to blanch noodles and beansprouts in small batches for individual servings, using the same blanching liquid. A small wire sieve would suffice but the small loops on the rim tend to get in the way.

WOKS

Although it is possible to cook oriental foods in an ordinary saucepan, having a wok makes it easier to cook certain dishes such as noodles and stirfries, especially when you have a gas ring. The conical base requires minimal oil for frying and the wide mouth allows you room to manoeuvre bulky items like noodles and vegetables. The rounded base is engineered to allow the flames to encircle the sides so that the food is cooked faster on the evenly heated surfaces. Finally the large surface area allows for rapid evaporation so that stirfried foods are not stewing in excess liquid.

The wok has also other applications. It can be converted into a steamer with the help of a trivet and a lid, and is also an ideal pan for deepfrying as its conical base allows for the minimal use of oil.

Choose a wok with a long handle rather than one with loop handles on either side. You will need one hand to stir and add the ingredients whilst the long handle allows you a better grip, away from the flames, to keep the wok in place and for tossing the food.

The term 'rempah' is used extensively in this book to mean the spice mixture that goes to make a particular dish. In most cases, the rempah is made up of fresh ingredients like onions, ginger, garlic, lemon grass and galanggal which have to be pulverised to a smooth paste before cooking. It is therefore essential to invest in a mini food processor and a liquidiser for grinding spices, and if you insist on grinding your own powdered spices like coriander, cumin and fennel, a coffee mill. I suggest a mini food processor like the Moulinex because the quantities involved are not sufficient to fill the bowl in a larger food processor and the ingredients tend to cling to the sides instead of falling into the middle to allow the blades to chop and slice. Consequently it is difficult to achieve the degree of fineness that is required.

For this reason, the liquidiser is much better as the jug surrounding the blades is narrower. The problem arises when the rempah has to be fairly dry because in most cases they are to be fried in oil and a watery rempah would impede this procedure. For one thing the liquid lowers the temperature of the oil and the rempah ends up being boiled rather than fried, and for another the combination of oil and water causes the mixture to splatter. This is not only hazardous but you want the rempah to stay in the pot, not on your walls, bodies and work surfaces. The mini food processor achieves both criteria and is therefore ideal.

As the liquid content in onions is high, adding chopped onions first with scant water should produce sufficient liquid to help process the other ingredients. The liquid could be strained off and pressed through a sieve and reused to grind the drier ingredients like lemon grass, galanggal, chillies and nuts. As in some cases the amount of ingredients to be ground may not fit in the jug or bowl all in one go, you may have to grind in batches and the following order is suggested:

Onions (strained to collect excess liquid); lemon grass (squeezed through sieve to collect liquid); galanggal (squeezed through sieve to collect liquid); ginger; chillies; garlic; candlenuts.

Blachan should always be added last because it is messy to remove. Always ensure there is enough liquid in the liquidiser to facilitate grinding, whether from the previous batch or added water.

Another trick is to use oil instead of water in a liquidiser but of course only as much oil as is necessary to fry the rempah without making it greasy.

Do not use oil if you intend to use the squeezing and straining method as the presence of oil would make it impossible to squeeze the ground ingredients. It would be necessary to reduce the amount of oil to be used for stirfrying as oil has already been incorporated into the rempah.

All the ingredients to be ground should be sliced as finely as possible so as to put less strain on the motor. It is essential that fibrous rhizomes such as galanggal and turmeric, ginger and lemon grass are finely sliced across the grain or you will end up with a ball of furry fibres. Onions should also be sliced across the grain in rings. Candlenuts and peanuts should first be ground separately in a bigger machine like the food processor. The coursely chopped nuts can then be ground to a paste in the blender with the rest of the ingredients.

If powdered spices are used, these should be folded into the 'wet' ground mixture to complete the rempah.

With the above tips you should find that the task of making rempah is not as awesome as you may think. It is after all the hardest part of the recipe, the rest is just a question of timing and adding.

Prepare all your ingredients before actually beginning to cook so that they are at hand to be added in the appropriate sequence.

Good luck and have fun.

STARTERS AND SOUPS

FRESH POPIAH

SATAY

POPIAH GORENG

LARB

UDANG GORENG

NGOH HIANG

PORK & PRAWN WANTUNS

WANTUN UDANG

SIU MAI

WANTUN SOUP

TUNGHOON SOUP

BAKWAN KEPITING

WATERCRESS, MINT AND SPARERIB SOUP

TULANG BABI MASAK KIAMCHYE

INGREDIENTS
1 packet 10in spring roll pastry

FILLING
14oz (375g) tinned bamboo shoot strips
10oz (275g) grated carrots
8oz (225g) finely shredded white cabbage
3 shallots, finely chopped
3 cloves garlic, finely chopped
2 dsp tauceo, mashed with a fork
2 dsp sugar
$^1/_2$ tsp salt, to taste
3 dsp cooking oil

GARNISHES
1lb (450g) cooked peeled prawns
2 hard boiled eggs, chopped
8oz (225g) cooked crab meat (optional)
8oz (225g) Chinese sausage (steamed for 10
minutes) or salami, finely chopped
$^1/_2$ cucumber, cut into julienne strips
8oz (225g) beansprouts, blanched and drained
1 lettuce, rinsed and patted dry on paper towel
1 bunch fresh coriander leaves, trimmed, washed
and patted dry on towel
6 cloves garlic, crushed
6oz (175g) ground roasted peanuts
6 red chillies, pounded into a paste or ground in
mini food processor
1 cup thick sweet soya sauce

SERVES
6-8

PREPARATION
45 minutes

F R E S H   P O P I A H

This Nonya style spring roll is served fresh without frying. A vast array of ingredients
go to make this delicious spring roll. Nonya households often serve this during lunch
parties when all the ingredients are laid out in decorative dishes in the middle of the
table and guests roll their own, helping themselves to all the bits and pieces that go in,
somewhat like serving Peking duck. It would be a novel way of serving lunch if you
haven't done it before, and great fun.

METHOD
1. Heat cooking oil in wok or large deep saucepan and lightly
brown chopped onions and garlic.

2. Add tauceo and season with sugar and salt to taste.

3. Add vegetables and stir to mix evenly. Cook for 5 minutes until
vegetables have softened. Set aside to cool.

4. Drain on colander until ready to use.

TO ASSEMBLE
Put vegetable filling into a large bowl and all garnishes into suitably
sized individual bowls or saucers.

Take one sheet of spring roll pastry and place on large plate.
Spread a thin layer of thick soya sauce in the centre of the pancake; a tiny bit of fresh garlic and a thin layer of chilli paste according to taste.

Put one piece of lettuce on top and 1 tablespoon of vegetable
filling on top of that. Sprinkle with chopped nuts, chopped egg, a
few flakes of crab meat, cooked prawns, Chinese sausage, bean
sprouts, coriander leaves etc. Bring bottom edge over the filling
and tuck under to keep in place then bring the sides half way
towards the middle. Roll away from you until the spring roll is
completely covered.

Cut the cylindrical roll into 4 or eat as a roll with fingers.

SATAY

INGREDIENTS

2lb (900g) meat (pork tenderloin, fillet steak, lamb or chicken)

80 8in Bamboo skewers

5 cloves garlic
3 stalks lemon grass, finely sliced
1in galanggal
1in ginger
Blended into a liquidiser with 2 tbsp cooking oil and 1 tbsp dark soya sauces

3 tbsp coriander powder
1 tsp cumin
$\frac{1}{2}$ tsp fennel powder
$\frac{1}{2}$ tsp ground white pepper
$\frac{1}{2}$ tsp turmeric powder

SERVES

6-8

PREPARATION

45 minutes

Can be made with beef, lamb, chicken or pork. Leaving a small amount of fat on the meat adds moisture and flavour and the charred fat is quite delicious.

Satay is best barbecued outdoors over charcoal as electric grilling is less flavoursome and it is difficult to stop the bamboo skewers from burning. Skewering the meats onto iron rods is one solution but the traditional and aesthetic presentation is lost.

METHOD

1. Slice meat into strips of 1in x $\frac{1}{2}$in thickness.

2. Marinate meat with blended fresh ingredients and powdered ingredients.

3. Add 2 tbsp sugar and 1 tsp salt to taste.

4. Thread meat onto skewers, adding 4-5 pieces of meat per skewer.

5. Leave to marinate on the skewers for at least 2 hours.

6. Preheat the grill to high and turn every few minutes to prevent burning, brushing with a basting mixture of half oil and half water until the meat is cooking. This might take anything between 2-10 minutes depending on the type of meat used. Beef would take less cooking time than say pork or chicken.

7. Serve with cucumber, pressed rice cakes and spicy peanut sauce (see page 132).

INGREDIENTS
1 packet 10in spring roll pastry
1 tbsp plain flour blended with a little water to
make a thick paste
oil for deep frying

FILLING:
14oz (375g) tinned bamboo shoot strips, boiled
in water and drained
12oz (350g) carrots, grated
$^1/_4$ white cabbage, finely sliced
10oz (275g) cooked peeled prawns
2 tbsp tauceo (preserved yellow beans) mashed
with a fork
1 tbsp sugar
$^1/_2$ tsp ground white pepper
1 medium onion, finely chopped
5 cloves garlic, finely chopped
3 dsp cooking oil
1 dsp light soya sauce

SERVES
6-8

PREPARATION
45 minutes

POPIAH GORENG
Fried spring rolls.

METHOD
1. Heat oil in wok and lightly brown chopped onions and garlic.

2. Add tauceo, sugar, soya sauce, salt and pepper and mix well.

3. Add bamboo shoots, carrots and white cabbage and mix well.

4. Keep stirring over medium heat for a further 5 minutes to cook vegetables.

5. Add prawns to vegetables unless you wish to keep some aside for vegans. Mix well and cook for a further minute or two.

6. Remove from heat and set aside to cool. Drain excess liquid over colander.

TO ASSEMBLE SPRING ROLLS
1. Tear off 2 sheets together. Lay on a clean flat surface with a pointed end towards you.

2. Put 2 tablespoons of well-drained filling across the lower half of the pastry. If prawns are to be added separately, these can be distributed on top of the filling at this stage.

3. Pick up the bottom point and bring it across the filling, tucking it tightly under the filling, squeezing out as much air as possible. Fold the right point into the centre half way across the spring roll and repeat with the left point. Finish rolling away from you towards the top point and seal with the flour paste. Repeat until fillings are used up.

4. Deepfry for three minutes until golden brown and serve with chilli and garlic sauce or sweet soya sauce.

Spring Rolls make ideal starters and cocktail food. The Nonya version uses tauceo (fermented yellow beans) which gives it a distinctive flavour. The ready-made pastry is wonderfully crisp and not at all greasy when deepfried.

INGREDIENTS
2 tbsp water
8oz (225g) breast of chicken, thinly sliced and minced in a food processor
1 stalk lemon grass, finely sliced
1 heaped tbsp fresh coriander leaves, finely chopped
$^1/_2$ fresh chilli (or less)
3 dsp lemon juice
1 dsp fish sauce
pinch of salt
1 tsp sugar
Selected leaves from the centre of an iceberg lettuce, or use little gems, or 4 tomato casings. Sprigs of coriander leaves to garnish.

SERVES
4

PREPARATION
15 minutes

L A R B

Not exactly a Singaporean or Nonya dish, Larb is a Laotian dish which I first tasted in a restaurant in Brussels run by Laotian boat refugees. So taken by its delicacy, I served it to various regulars in my Fulham restaurant.

METHOD

1. Finely chop fresh coriander leaves, chillies and lemon grass in a mini food processor or mill and pulse for a further 5 seconds . Season with lemon juice, fish sauce, sugar and salt to taste. Set aside.

2. Bring $^1/_2$ cup of water to the boil in a small saucepan with a pinch of salt. Add minced chicken, stirring continuously to break up the lumps and cook for 5 minutes until all the water is absorbed and the chicken is fairly dry. Add coriander dressing and mix well.

TO SERVE
Arrange lettuce boats (or alternative receptacle) on a plate and spoon heaps of minced chicken with dressing onto them. Garnish with coriander leaves and slices of tomato for colour.

INGREDIENTS

1lb (450g) tiger prawns (Size 8-12)
2 dsp light soya
1 dsp sesame oil
3 tbsp corn flour for coating
$\frac{1}{2}$ tsp ground white pepper
1 dsp sherry or brandy (optional)
4 cups cooking oil for deep frying

SERVES

Allow at least 2 prawns per person as a starter

PREPARATION

10 minutes

UDANG GORENG

Deep fried tiger prawns marinated in light soya and sesame oil

You can serve this dish as a starter or main course. It is such a simple dish and so easy to prepare, yet utterly delicious. It always brings out the 'oohs' and 'aahs' when they are brought to the dining table.

Tiger prawns are available in different sizes. Size 8-12 means you would get 8-12 prawns to the pound, 21-25 means 21-25 prawns in the pound and so on.

Under size 6 are impressively enormous prawns but I find them to be quite tough. For the purposes of this recipe, the prawns should be at least sized 8-12 as prawns inevitably shrink during frying.

METHOD

1. Peel tiger prawns but leave the tail on. Make a slit on the back and de-vein. Pat dry on kitchen towel.

2. Marinate prawns with seasonings - soya sauce, sesame oil, salt and pepper, and sherry or brandy if used. Marinate for at least 15 minutes.

3. Roll marinated prawns in cornflour.

4. Heat cooking oil in wok or deep fryer and deep fry coated prawns, a few at a time. Adding too many prawns to the oil would lower the temperature of the oil and the prawns would not be crisp.

5. Deepfry for 2-3 minutes until golden brown. Drain on paper towels and serve immediately, garnished with fresh salads such as cucumber, tomatoes, or shredded iceberg lettuce and a sprig of parsley. Delicious eaten with a chilli and garlic dipping sauce - see recipe on page 134.

INGREDIENTS

1lb (450g) minced pork
8oz (225g) green prawns, shelled and minced
6oz (175g) cooked crab meat (optional)
1 small onion, finely chopped
8oz (225g) water chestnuts, finely chopped
2 eggs, lightly beaten
1 dsp sugar
1 tsp salt
$\frac{1}{2}$ tsp ground white pepper
1 heaped tsp fivespice powder
1 dsp light soya sauce
1 dsp dark soya sauce

8oz (225g) dried beancurd sheets
Oil for deep frying

SERVES
6-8

PREPARATION
45 minutes

N GOH HIAN G
Meat rolls in beancurd pastry

The chewy texture of dried beancurd sheets is deepfried to produce flavourful crisp rolls with the added crunchiness of waterchestnuts. Fivespice powder lends a delicate spicy flavour.
Photograph on page 16.

METHOD

1. Cut the dried beancurd wrappers into 8in x 8in squares. Soak in warm water and lay flat on a clean damp cloth.

2. Combine the minced pork and prawns with all the seasoning ingredients and lightly beaten egg.

3. Lay a trimmed sheet of beancurd pastry on the work surface with one pointed end towards you. Sprinkle with water to soften the skin.

4. Put 2 heaped tbsp of filling mixture in the middle of each wrapper. Pick up the bottom point and bring it across the filling, tucking it tightly under the filling. Bring both sides towards the middle and roll away towards the top and seal edges with water.

5. Steam the rolls for 15 minutes to cook the filling. They can then be set aside until ready to serve.

TO SERVE

6. Deep fry in medium hot oil for 5 minutes until the filling is hot and the skin is brown and crispy.

7. Drain onto paper towels. Cut across 1-1$\frac{1}{2}$in apart and serve on a bed of iceberg lettuce or sliced cucumber with sweet chilli sauce or sweet soya sauce.

INGREDIENTS

8oz (225g) minced pork
8oz (225g) green prawns, shelled and de-veined
1 tbsp light soya sauce
1 dsp sesame oil
1 dsp sugar
pinch of salt and pepper
1 tbsp chopped coriander leaves (optional)
10oz (275g) wantun pastry (approx. 50 sheets) -
makes 50 wantuns

SERVES

6-8

PREPARATION

20 minutes

PORK AND PRAWN WANTUNS

Photograph page 21.

METHOD

1. Put above ingredients except wantun pastry into food processor and pulse for 5-10 seconds until well mixed. If using sliced pork steaks, mince pork separately in food processor before adding all other ingredients.

2. Before making up the wantuns, taste mixture, cooking a small quantity by dropping it in deepfryer or boiling water. Adjust seasoning to desired taste by adding more light soya sauce or sugar if necessary.

3. To wrap in pastry, place a teaspoonful of filling in the middle of the pastry square. Lightly dab cold water round the meat onto the pastry. Bring edges together and lightly squeeze to seal.

TO COOK

The wantuns can then be deepfried in medium hot oil for 5 minutes and kept warm in an oven. They are best served straight from the fryer. Serve with chilli and garlic dip or sweet plum syrup.

WANTUN PRAWNS

INGREDIENTS

12-18 tiger prawns

1 tbsp light soya
1 dsp sesame oil
1 dsp sugar
pinch of salt and pepper

24-36 wantun pastry sheets

SERVES

6-8

PREPARATION

10 minutes

METHOD

Peel tiger prawns leaving tail on. Use 21-25 sized prawns for best effect. Allow at least 2 per person.

Peel and de-vein the prawns, leaving the tails on. Marinate in the same soya/sesame mixture with sugar and pepper to taste. Wrap in wantun pastry using 2 sheets of pastry per prawn, leaving tail unwrapped. Make sure the prawns are well sealed by just dabbing with cold water or the pastry will unfold in the frying process.

Serve with sweet chilli and garlic sauce.

INGREDIENTS

8oz (225g) minced pork
8oz (225g) green tiger prawns (peeled and deveined)
1 tbsp light soya sauce
1 dsp sugar
$1/_2$ tsp salt and pepper to taste
1 tsp sesame oil
2oz (50g) water chestnuts, finely chopped
3-4 dried Chinese mushrooms, soaked in hot water to soften and chopped

6oz (175g) wantun pastry - makes about 30

SERVES
6-8

PREPARATION
20 minutes

INGREDIENTS - SOUP

2 pints (1.2 litres) chicken/vegetable stock
1 tbsp light soya sauce
1 tbsp fish sauce
1 tsp salt
pinch of ground white pepper
3 slices ginger
1 tbsp spring onions, finely sliced into rings to garnish.

SERVES
6

PREPARATION
20 minutes

SIU MAI
Steamed pork and prawn dumplings

This is a dim sum dish that is ideal served as a starter. Make it when you have bought in a stack of wantun pastry and freeze for future use. You can also use the same filling for making into crispy pork and prawn wantuns, or dropped into boiling stock and served as wantun soup.

METHOD

1. Combine all ingredients except pastry and chop in food processor for 1 minute until finely chopped and mixed.

2. Trim round the square pastry to form circles. Put 1 dsp filling into the middle of wantun pastry and bring sides up to form a cup, pinching the sides all the way round to form pleats, exposing the filling at the top.

3. Brush each dumpling with a little oil to prevent sticking and steam for 10-15 minutes until cooked.

4. Delicious served with hoisin sauce and/or sweet chilli sauce (see recipe on page 135).

WANTUN SOUP

METHOD

1. Make pork and prawn wantuns (method and ingredients as described above) without frying as the wantuns should be boiled instead.

2. Cook prepared wantuns in a saucepan of boiling water for 5 minutes. Remove with a slotted spoon and drain on colander.

3. Bring stock to boil, flavour with ginger slices and season with fish sauce, light soya sauce and salt. Add cooked wantuns and serve garnished with spring onions and a dash of white pepper.

Wantun pastry is as versatile as pasta dough. It can be filled with various fillings and wrapped in imaginative ways for deepfrying, steaming or simply boiled in soups.

INGREDIENTS

4oz (110g) glass noodles
(soaked in hot water to soften)
3 pints (1½ litres) chicken stock
6oz (175g) pork steaks
4oz (110g) green prawns
4 dsp light soya sauce
1 dsp salt
dash of ground white pepper
1 tbsp chopped coriander leaves
2 slices fresh ginger
1 tsp sesame oil

GARNISHES

2 stalks spring onions or coriander leaves
Fried onion rings

SERVES

4-6

PREPARATION

20 minutes

T U N G H O O N   S O U P
Pork and prawn flavoured soup with glass noodles

Glass noodles, also known as cellophane or transparent noodles, are made from the starch of mung bean flour and sold in dried form. They should be soaked in hot water for 8-10 minutes before use and are popularly added to soups rather than stirfried. In Thailand they are served as a salad when combined with prawns and other seafood in a hot and sour dressing.

In their dried form, they are tough and wiry and difficult to separate without the use of kitchen scissors. I find it easier to buy them in 2oz bundles although the larger packs are more economical.

METHOD

1. Mince pork steaks and shelled prawns in a food processor seasoned with 2 dsp light soya sauce, 1 tsp sesame oil, salt and pepper and coriander leaves.

2. Bring chicken stock or water to the boil in a stock pot with ginger slices and drop in tiny balls of the minced pork and prawn mixture. Skim off any scum that rises to the top. Simmer for 10 minutes.

3. Season soup with light soya, fish sauce, salt and pepper to taste.

4. Just before serving, add a handful of the drained transparent noodles to each bowl, topped with fried onion rings and chopped spring onions.

Tip: *Fried onion rings stay crisp for weeks if they are well drained on kitchen paper soon after frying and kept in an air-tight container - ready for use on soups and fried noodles*

BAKWAN KEPITING
Crab and pork soup

The Chinese fondness for soups at every meal is evident in the number of recipes that exist, both simple and complex. This is a soup that is traditionally served at weddings and other auspicious occasions.

INGREDIENTS

8oz (225g) minced pork
8oz (225g) white crab meat
1 egg
4 cloves garlic, chopped
2oz (50g) bamboo shoots, finely chopped
1 dsp sugar
salt to taste
dash of ground white pepper
1 dsp light soya
3 tbsp cooking oil

FOR THE SOUP:

3 pints (1$\frac{1}{2}$ litres) water or chicken stock
2 slices fresh ginger
4oz (110g) bamboo shoots, finely sliced
1 dsp sherry
2 tbsp light soya
1 dsp fish sauce
2 tsp salt
1 tsp sugar

GARNISHES

Fried onion rings
1 tbsp chopped coriander leaves or spring onions

SERVES

6

PREPARATION

30 minutes

METHOD

1. Heat 3 tbsp cooking oil and lightly brown chopped garlic. Remove garlic and set aside.

2. Mince pork in food processor and add the egg, crab meat and bamboo shoots. Season with fried garlic, light soya, salt, sugar and pepper. Pulse for 10 seconds until well mixed. Grease the palm of your hands with cooking oil and form into balls.

3. In stock pot, bring chicken stock to the boil and add 2 slices of ginger.

4. Drop the balls of crab and pork mixture into boiling stock, skimming off any scum that rises to the top.

5. Add sliced bamboo shoots.

6. Season with light soya, fish sauce, sherry, salt and pepper and simmer for 15 minutes over medium heat.

6. Serve into individual bowls and garnish with chopped coriander leaves and fried onion rings.

INGREDIENTS

2lbs (900g) spare ribs, chopped into bite sized pieces
2 bunches watercress, washed and trimmed
2oz (50g) fresh mint
2 tbsp light soya sauce
$\frac{1}{2}$in fresh ginger, thinly sliced
dash of ground white pepper
4 pints (3 litres) water
I dsp salt to taste

SERVES

4-6

PREPARATION

15 minutes

WATERCRESS MINT AND SPARE RIB SOUP

This is a deliciously fragrant soup served in the Chinese style with the main course. There is no reason why you shouldn't serve this in the European fashion as a soup course.

METHOD

1. Bring water to the boil in a deep soup pan with the ginger.

2. Add spare ribs and salt and simmer for 30 minutes, removing scum as it rises, especially during the first 15 minutes.

3. Cook until spare ribs are tender.

4. Add watercress and mint, soya sauce and seasonings and cook for 3 minutes.

5. Serve onto individual bowls or soup tureen and sprinkle with a dash of ground white pepper just before serving.

Soups served in Chinese and southeast Asian meals are seldom served as starters. They are normally served as part of the main courses to "wet" the rice and refresh the palate, especially if most of the main dishes served happen to be fried or barbecued.

INGREDIENTS

2lbs (900g) pork spare ribs (ask your butcher to chop it into bite size pieces)
16oz (450g) tin of kiamchye, drained and cut into 2in lengths
1in fresh ginger, lightly crushed
4 pints (3 litres) water
4 preserved sour plums (optional)
2 tomatoes, quartered
1 tsp salt
1 dsp sugar
$\frac{1}{2}$ tsp ground white pepper

SERVES

4-6

PREPARATION

15 minutes

TULANG BABI
MASAK KIAMCHYE
Pork spare rib and salted mustard green soup

Unlike western cuisine, most soups served in Chinese and southeast Asian meals are seldom served as starters. They are normally served as part of the main courses to "wet" the rice and refresh the palate, especially if most of the main dishes served happen to be fried or barbecued and "sauceless". Each diner is given a separate bowl to serve himself from and the soup, with all its bits is drunk throughout the main course.

The pickled salted cabbage imparts a special flavour to the soup. In the far east Kiamchye is bought loose from the market soaked in large basins of brine but in the west you can buy it canned from Chinese supermarkets.
Photograph on page 107.

METHOD

1. Bring water to the boil in a large stock pot and add spare ribs and ginger.

2. Skim off the scum as it rises to the top until the soup is clear.

3. Simmer for 30 minutes and add kiamchye, preserved sour plums, and tomatoes.

4. Season with salt, pepper and sugar to taste.

5. Cook for a further 10 minutes and serve with a dash of pepper.

VEGETABLES

CHAP CHYE

SAYUR LODEH

TAUHU GORENG

TAUGEH CHAR KIAMCHYE

KACHANG PANJANG TITEK

SAMBAL KANGKONG

ROJAK

GADO

SAMBAL KIMCHIAM

TAUHU TAUCEO

ACHAR PINANG

SAMBAL BINDI

In the Far East we are spoilt for choice when it comes to green leafy vegetables all year round. Some of these are now being cultivated here or imported by air and I thought it would be useful to describe them in greater detail so that the next time you visit a Chinese supermarket you need not be completely ignorant of the vegetables that are available. Some, like the pak choi and choi sum, have also made their way to the large supermarket chains.

VEGETABLES

CHINESE WHITE CABBAGE (PAK CHOI)
There are several varieties of this favourite Chinese vegetable. They can best be identified by their two-tone leaves and long white stalks. Although they can be eaten raw, they are best served stirfried with a few slices of ginger, a clove of chopped garlic and flavoured with oyster sauce.

CHINESE GREENS (CHOI SUM)
Arguably one of the best Chinese cabbages, the tender leaves and stems are used in a variety of dishes. Easily distinguished by its bright green leaves with bright yellow flowers and pale green stems, its prolific supply says much for its popularity. It is added to soups and noodles, casseroles and stir fried on its own or combined with shrimps and meats. It has a sweet flavour and a crisp texture and is considered by the Chinese to have the most neutral nutritional value - neither 'cooling' nor 'heating' properties, and therefore safe to eat in abundance. In stirfry dishes, it cooks within a few minutes and maintains its crispness and bright green appearance. The thick stalk at the end should be discarded.

ANGLED LOOFAH
This vegetable is easily identified by the prominent longitudinal ridges on the coarse and thick green skin. Somewhat earthy in flavour, the sponge-like texture of this squash soaks up any added flavouring. It is therefore excellent with oyster sauce. It can be steamed or added to omelettes and soups or casseroled, and is very versatile. Use a vegetable peeler to remove the outer skin.

KANG KONG (WATER CONVOLVULUS)
It has a light green colour and looks like spinach with long spear-shaped leaves but the stems have air pockets which pop when squeezed. The stems remain crunchy when cooked. A favourite vegetable among Southeast Asians and used in stirfry dishes. Look out for Nonya recipes in which they are spiced up and varied with coconut milk. Considered a 'cooling' food. Fairly easy to come across in recent years in Chinese and Thai supermarkets. Extremely cheap in Asia but expensive in Europe as they are imported by air.

OKRA (LADIES FINGERS, GUMBO)

This vegetable is a favourite with Indians, West Indians and southeast Asians. Ranging from 2in-4in in length they are green pods encasing tiny white seeds with a slimy sap. The slime does disappear after prolonged cooking. Tends to be stringy if harvested late although the longer they are left before picking, the bigger they are. It is best therefore to choose them small but check for freshness by snapping off the tip. They should also feel fairly soft to the touch as opposed to hard and hairy. Although the above description may not sound too appetising, ladies fingers are quite delicious when properly cooked, whether in the Indian or Nonya and Malay recipes given in this book.

INGREDIENTS

4oz (110g) bamboo shoot slices
8oz (225g) green prawns (size 21-25) or use cooked peeled prawns
2 sticks dried beancurd soaked in hot water for 30 minutes to soften. Cut into 1$\frac{1}{2}$in lengths.
8oz (225g) white cabbage, cut into 1in squares
1 oz wood ears (soaked to soften and chopped)
2 squares fried beancurd, diced
1oz (25g) lily buds, knotted and soaked to soften
2 carrots, sliced
4 dried Chinese mushrooms, soaked to soften and thinly sliced

1 tbsp tauceo (fermented yellow beans)
1 tbsp sugar
1 tsp salt
2 pints (1.2 litres) water or stock
3 dsp cooking oil

REMPAH
4 oriental shallots
3 cloves garlic

GARNISHES
1 dsp spring onions, finely chopped
2oz (50g) glass noodles, blanched to soften and drained

SERVES
6-8

PREPARATION
20 minutes

CHAP CHYE
Vegetarian stew with beancurd in yellow bean sauce

Literally translated from Chinese, it means "ten vegetables" and should have that many different items to make this highly nutritious vegetarian stew. It is the main staple for Buddhist monks, who are vegans. The Nonya version uses prawns and pork to sweeten and enrich the dish but they can easily be omitted if wished.
Photograph (bottom) page 31.

METHOD
1. Prepare vegetable ingredients.

2. Roughly chop shallots and garlic in mini food processor for 10 seconds, or roughly pound with pestle and mortar.

3. Heat oil in large deep saucepan and lightly brown onions and garlic mixture until fragrant. Add tauceo and stir to prevent sticking.

4. Top up with water or stock and add vegetables, lily buds, wood ears, carrots, cabbage and beancurd sticks.

5. Season with sugar, salt and pepper to taste. Bring to the boil.

6. Simmer on medium heat for 10 minutes until cabbage is tender. Add cooked prawns, if used, during the last five minutes of cooking.

7. Transfer to serving bowl and sprinkle with blanched glass noodles.

8. Garnish with spring onions.

INGREDIENTS

$^1/_4$ white cabbage, cut into $1^1/_2$in pieces

2oz (50g) kenyan beans, top and tailed and cut into $1^1/_2$in lengths

2 carrots, peeled and cut into strips or thinly sliced into rings

4oz (110g) cooked peeled prawns or dried prawns soaked in warm water to soften

2oz (50g) tunghoon (transparent noodles) soaked in water to soften and drained

2oz (50g) coconut powder mixed with 1 cup of water

1 tsp salt (to taste)

3 dsp cooking oil

2 cakes beancurd, deep fried for 10 minutes and quartered (optional)

2 pints (1.2 litres) vegetable stock or hot water

Note: Any combination of vegetables can be used, including baby corn, bamboo shoots, broccoli, cauliflower, leeks, mooli and aubergines.

REMPAH

2-3 red chillies, thinly sliced

$^1/_2$ medium red onion or 8 shallots

$^1/_4$in blachan

6 candlenuts or 1 dsp ground candlenuts

1 clove garlic

$^1/_4$ tsp tumeric

Liquidise into a fine paste with 2-3 dsp of cooking oil.

SERVES

6-8

PREPARATION

30 minutes

SAYUR LODEH

The variety of vegetables used makes this dish particularly appealing to vegetarians. The addition of prawns, dried or fresh, adds extra flavour but can be omitted if desired.
Traditionally served fairly 'soupy' as an accompaniment to rice and fried fish or dry meat dishes. When served with Nasi Tinday, and Serunding it constitutes a meal in itself.
Photograph (top) page 31.

METHOD

1. Heat 2 dsp cooking oil and fry the rempah in a large deep saucepan over high heat until fragrant and the oil starts to separate.

2. Add dried prawns, if used, at this stage. Season with salt and top up with stock or boiling water.

3. Add vegetables in order (those taking the longest to cook being the first to be added). Simmer until all the vegetables are cooked through *al dente*.

4. Just before serving, add coconut cream, glass noodles and deepfried beancurd. Add cooked prawns, if used, at this stage.

5. Bring to the boil and serve hot.

INGREDIENTS

6 beancurd cakes, deep fried until golden brown
8oz (225g) beansprouts, blanched
$1/_2$ cucumber, deseeded and cut into julienne strips
cooking oil for deep frying

PEANUT SAUCE

8oz (225g) roasted peanuts, chopped coarsely in processor
1 tbsp brown sugar
2-3 red chillies, finely sliced (reduce as necessary)
3 cloves garlic
$1/_2$ tsp salt
1 tbsp dark soya sauce
1 dsp vinegar
$1/_2$ cup boiling water

SERVES
4-6

PREPARATION
15 minutes

TAUHU GORENG
Fried beancurd with beansprouts served with peanut sauce

An ideal vegetarian dish, beancurd is packed with protein. It is relatively tasteless but some like it because of its soft texture which can be improved by deep frying, giving it a crispy crust. Combined with the crunchiness of a piquant peanut sauce and crisp beansprouts, both texture and taste is transformed into a robust dish that gets your jaws into action.

METHOD
1. Cut beancurd into 3in squares, Deep fry in hot oil two at a time until goldlen brown and crispy. Drain on kitchen towel and keep warm.

2. Finely chop chillies and garlic in mini food processor.

3. Combine chopped nuts, chilli and garlic paste and hot water, vinegar, soya sauce and salt in a separate saucepan and mix well to form a runny sauce and simmer on low heat to keep warm.

4. Blanch beansprouts in a pint of boiling water for a minute and drain on colander.

TO ASSEMBLE
Cut fried beancurd cake into quarters and put on a serving dish. Sprinkle blanched beansprouts and julienned cucumber strips on top and pour hot peanut sauce to serve.

There are two ways of serving this dish. The beancurd can either be cut into one inch squares and topped with the beansprouts and cucumber, or cut into two triangles. Make a slit through the middle of each triangle to form a pouch and stuff with the vegetables. The peanut sauce is then poured over the stuffed beancurd.

INGREDIENTS

1lb (450g) fresh beansprouts, rinsed and drained
6oz (175g) (kiamchye) pickled mustard greens, soaked in water
$^1/_2$in ginger, cut into julienne strips
1 large red chilli, finely sliced
2 cloves garlic, finely sliced
1 dsp sugar
pinch of salt and pepper
2 dsp cooking oil

SERVES

4-6

PREPARATION

10 minutes

INGREDIENTS

1lb (450g) long beans, cut into 2in lengths
6oz (175g) small prawns, or cooked peeled prawns
$1^1/_2$ pints (850ml) water or stock
4oz (110g) coconut powder, dissolved in 1 cup hot water
2 tsp salt, to taste

REMPAH

3 large red chillies
1 small red onion, chopped
4 candlenuts
1 dsp blachan

SERVES

4-6

PREPARATION

15 minutes

TAUGEH CHAR KIAMCHYE

Stirfried beansprouts with pickled mustard greens

METHOD

1. Finely slice mustard greens.

2. Heat oil in wok until smoking and lightly brown ginger and garlic slices. Add sliced chillies.

3. Add sliced kiamchye and stir to mix. Cook for a minute and season with sugar and salt to taste. Add beanspouts just before serving so that they will retain their crispness.

KACHANG PANJANG TITEK

A Nonya style spicy vegetable dish using long beans.

METHOD

1. Make rempah in liquidiser and grind to a fine paste.

2. Bring water to the boil and add rempah, and season with salt. Simmer for 10 minutes until rempah is cooked.

3. Add long beans and cook for 5 minutes to tenderise.

4. Add prawns and cook for 3 minutes until they turn pink.

5. Add coconut milk to thicken and adjust seasoning. Simmer for 5 minutes on low heat so as not to curdle coconut milk and serve in soup tureen.

Taugeh Char Kiamchye, bottom left, is a simple stirfry dish combining beanspouts with pickled mustard greens. Fresh beanspouts are easily available and inexpensive. Sprouted from mung beans, they are highly nutritious as the sprouting chemistry changes the starch in the seeds into vitamins and sugars. They are considered by Chinese nutritionists to have detoxifying properties and being 'cooling', are eaten to offset heated conditions in the body.

INGREDIENTS

1lb (450g) kangkong
8oz (225g) green prawns (size 21-25) or use
cooked peeled prawns
3 dsp cooking oil
1 dsp sugar
$\frac{1}{2}$ tsp salt to taste

REMPAH

4 shallots, finely sliced
2 cloves garlic, finely sliced
4 candlenuts, crushed
2 fresh red chillies or 6 dried chillies
1 tsp blachan
2 dsp cooking oil

SERVES

4

PREPARATION

20 minutes

SAMBAL KANGKONG

Water convolvulus stirfried with dried prawns in sambal sauce

If you can find water convolvulus in the Chinese and Thai supermarkets, do try this fabulous vegetable dish which is a favourite among Southeast Asians. The stems of the kangkong are wonderfully crisp whilst the spearshaped leaves are tender like spinach. If you are not too keen on the spicy blachan sauce then stirfry with garlic and they make delicious greens. I hope you will be adventurous and try the following recipe.
Photograph (right) page 35.

METHOD

1. Wash kangkong and separate the soft green leaves from the stems. Cut stems into 2in lengths. Drain on colander.

2. Make rempah in mini food processor as it requires no liquid at all. If using liquidiser, add cooking oil and scant water to facilitate grinding.

3. Heat 3 dsp cooking oil in wok or large saucepan and stirfry rempah until fragrant.

4. Add prawns and stir to prevent sticking and burning until prawns turn pink.

5. Season with sugar and salt and add stems of kangkong. Cook for 2 minutes before adding the leaves which will only require a minute or so to cook.

6. Adjust seasoning and serve.

INGREDIENTS
VEGETABLES
$1/2$ cucumber
$1/2$ pineapple
8oz (225g) bangkwang (yam bean) (or substitute sweet potatoes)
8oz (225g) fresh beansprouts, blanched
4oz (110g) kangkong, cut into 2in lengths and blanched
4oz (110g) fried beancurd, diced
1 carrot, peeled and thinly sliced

SAUCE
1 tbsp tamarind, soaked in $1/2$ cup boiling water to extract juice
8oz (225g) roasted peanuts, chopped
1 tbsp sugar
2 tbsp heyko
1 dsp sambal blachan (optional or use 1 dsp chopped fresh red chillies)
$1/2$ tsp salt

SERVES
4-6

PREPARATION
20 minutes

R o j a K

A Malay salad that uses Heyko (dried prawn paste) as a base. This is your chance to use Bangkwang at its best when you see them in the Chinese supermarkets. A salad dish that is enjoyed on its own as a snack, it is usually bought from a hawker stall and in the good old days, served in a dried leaf but nowadays is served in a polystyrene bowl or melamine plate.

Try serving this as a fresh salad starter. Use firm textured tart fruits like sour granny smith apples, green mangoes or green papayas as alternatives. In southeast Asia, green bananas and raw sweet potatoes are also used to make this salad.

METHOD
1. Prepare vegetables as above. Deseed cucumber and cut into $1/2$in slices. If using fresh pineapples, remove core and cut into bite-size pieces. Dice fried beancurd into $1/2$in cubes. Peel yam bean and cut into thin slices. Blanch kangkong and beansprouts and drain over colander.

2. Combine sauce ingredients, except chopped peanuts, in a liquidiser and blend at high speed.

3. In a salad bowl, toss the prepared vegetables with the sauce ingredients and add ground peanuts.

Note: If yam beans are not available, substitute with one tart apple such as Granny Smiths and/or one carrot.

INGREDIENTS

VEGETABLES

8oz (225g) beansprouts

8oz (225g) white cabbage, finely shredded

2-3 carrots, shredded

1 cucumber, deseeded and cut into julienne strips

$^1/_2$ iceberg lettuce, finely shredded

6 eggs, hardboiled, cut into wedges

4 potatoes, boiled, peeled and sliced

8oz (225g) long beans or kenyan beans, topped and tailed and cut into 2in lengths

4 cakes beancurd, deep fried and diced

1 cake tempeh (fermented bean cake), deep fried and cut into $^1/_2$in strips (optional)

SAUCE

4 cups chopped roasted peanuts

1 tsp salt

2 tbsp sugar

1 tbsp tamarind, soaked in 1 cup boiling water to extract juice

4oz (110g) coconut powder, dissolved in 1 cup hot water

3 dsp cooking oil

1 cup water

REMPAH

3 large red chillies, finely sliced

1 medium onion, finely sliced

2 cloves garlic, finely sliced

6 candlenuts, crushed

1 dsp blachan

3 dsp cooking oil

SERVES

8 or more

PREPARATION

30 minutes

GADO GADO
Indonesian salad with spicy peanut sauce

This is a fairly substantial salad dish, rather like Salade Nicoise without the tuna, and is great for parties as it makes an impressive centrepiece.
The sauce can be made in advance and poured over the blanched salad vegetables when required.

METHOD

1. Blend rempah finely in mini food processor. If using liquidiser, use scant water to facilitate grinding

2. Heat 3 dsp cooking oil in saucepan and fry rempah until fragrant, stirring constantly to prevent sticking and burning.

3. Add remaining sauce ingredients - tamarind juice, sugar, coconut milk and salt, nuts and water. Simmer for 15 minutes over low heat until thickened. Keep hot.

4. Prepare vegetables and arrange decoratively on a large platter. Garnish with fried onion rings or prawn crackers. Pour hot peanut sauce over when ready to serve, or put into a separate bowl for individuals to help themselves.

INGREDIENTS

2oz (50g) golden needles (lily buds)
1lb (450g) tiger prawns (size 21-25) or use cooked peeled prawns
$^1/_2$ cucumber, deseeded and cut into julienne strips
1 red chilli, finely sliced

DRESSING

8oz (225g) coconut powder dissolved in 1 cup hot water
1 dsp sambal blachan (see page 134).
juice of 1 lime
1 tbsp sugar
$^1/_2$ tsp salt

SERVES

4-6

PREPARATION

30 minutes

SAMBAL KIMCHIAM
Prawn and golden needle salad in coconut dressing

A favourite among the old Nonyas. It is a deliciously rich dish and a novel way of serving prawns. Impress your friends with the use of golden needles - a new vegetable to savour.

METHOD

1. Prepare golden needles as follows. Remove hard stalk and tie into a knot. Rinse and boil in 1 pint of water for 5 minutes to soften. Drain.

2. If using green prawns, cook for 5-8 minutes until they turn pink. Keep warm and set aside.

3. Combine dressing ingredients in a separate bowl. Cook over a gentle heat and keep warm.

4. Arrange golden needles, julienned cucumbers and prawns on a platter and pour hot coconut dressing over the top. Garnish with thinly sliced red chillies.

INGREDIENTS

2 squares beancurd, deep fried and diced
8oz (225g) leek, trimmed and sliced
diagonally
4oz (110g) green prawns, peeled and
de-veined (use cooked prawns if this is
more convenient)
1 dsp dark soya sauce
1 dsp tauceo (fermented yellow beans)
1 dsp sugar
3 dsp cooking oil
1 tsp vinegar
salt and pepper to taste
$^1/_2$ cup water
1 cup oil for deep frying beancurd

GARNISHES

1 red chilli, finely sliced, 1 dsp chopped
coriander leaves

REMPAH

$^1/_2$ in ginger, thinly sliced
2 red chillies, thinly sliced
2 cloves garlic, thinly sliced
4 shallots or 1 medium onion

SERVES

4

PREPARATION

20 minutes

TAUHU TAUCEO

Fried beancurd with leeks.

I have always felt that leeks are a neglected vegetable. Not everyone's favourite but if cooked in an appetising way they could be converted. Highly nutritious and good for getting rid of winds in the system.

METHOD

1. Make rempah in a mini food processor. If using a liquidiser, add cooking oil to facilitate grinding.

2. Heat 3 dsp cooking oil in wok or saucepan and fry rempah until fragrant. Add tauceo and season with sugar, salt and pepper.

3. Add green prawns and cook for a minute before adding leeks. Cook for a further 3 minutes.

4. Add fried beancurd and stir to mix.

5. Transfer onto serving dish and garnish with sliced chillies and chopped coriander leaves.

The aromatic and distinctive flavour of tauceo, combined with ginger, chillies and garlic provides a delicious sauce for the otherwise bland beancurd. Leeks not only heighten the flavours but provide texture and colour

INGREDIENTS

2 cucumbers, deseeded and cut into 2in x $\frac{1}{2}$in strips

4 carrots, cut into 2in x $\frac{1}{2}$in strips

8oz (225g) white cabbage, cut into 1in pieces

6oz (175g) long beans (or use kenyan beans) cut into 2in lengths

8oz (225g) cauliflower, cut into florets

6oz (175g) raw peanuts, roasted and chopped

1 tbsp sesame seeds

REMPAH

10oz (275g) shallots

2 stalks lemon grass, finely sliced

$\frac{1}{2}$in galanggal, finely sliced

1in ginger, thinly sliced

1 tbsp ground turmeric

20 dried chillies or 2 tbsp ground chillies

5 tbsp cooking oil

12oz (330ml) malt vinegar

10oz (275ml) water

8oz (225g) sugar

2 tbsp salt

SERVES

10 or more as relish.

PREPARATION

60 minutes or more

ACHAR PINANG

A Nonya pickle of crunchy mixed vegetables in a spicy nutty sauce

The Nonya Achar is one of the most delectable dishes I can remember having but it is also one of the most labour intensive and involves days of sun drying the vegetables so that they maintain their crispness during the pickling process. Mounds of freshly cut cucumbers and carrots are reduced to a handful after they have been exposed to the hot tropical sun for a few days. My favourite ingredient in this pickle is chillies stuffed with sun-dried shredded green papaya.

Although it is a favourite relish, my mother only ever made achar during the Chinese New Year celebrations because of the work involved. It is only during the festive season that everyone's favourite dishes are prepared, no matter how arduous or expensive. It is undoubtedly a favourite time of year for children as they can enjoy being pampered with good food, new clothes and accessories, gifts of 'any pow' which are red envelopes containing money and a happy ambience all round as to be cross brings forth bad luck for the new year. Consequently children are seldom chastised for any wrongdoing.

For the mothers the period leading up to Chinese New Year is a hectic one as not only are there a hundred-and-one dishes to cook, cakes and sweetmeats to bake, the house has to be springcleaned from top to bottom and new clothes made or bought for the children. However, there is comfort in the thought that three days following Chinese New Year, no cooking is allowed and everyone lives on the leftovers. This is why they tend to cook to excess not only to cater for visiting guests but to cover for the period of rest.

Serving pickled vegetables to accompany the rich foods that are inevitably served also solves the problem of the lack of fresh vegetables during this period when the market is closed and whatever produce is available is unlikely to be fresh and of high quality. The pickles will last for up to a month if stored in a sterilised jar and kept cooled.

The following recipe is a simplified version. Instead of using solar energy, the cucumber and carrots (which have the highest water content) are dehydrated by salting and pressing.

METHOD

1. Cut deseeded cucumber into 2in x $\frac{1}{2}$in strips. Sprinkle with salt and tie into a muslin bag. Weight with a heavy object to remove excess moisture. Repeat with carrots.

2. Blanch white cabbage, beans and cauliflower in boiling water for 2 minutes, drain and set aside.

3. Prepare rempah in a liquidiser until fine.

4. Heat cooking oil in a wok or saucepan and fry rempah until it is fragrant and the oil is separated from the mixture.

5. Add vinegar, sugar, salt and top up with water. Bring to the boil and simmer for 5 minutes. Leave to cool.

6. Add sauce to blanched and prepared vegetables and toss with nuts and sesame seeds. Bottle in dry sterilised jars and seal when cooled.

Best served after 24 hours.

INGREDIENTS

1lb (450g) ladies fingers
4oz (110g) dried prawns, soaked in 1 cup boiling water to soften (substitute fresh prawns if desired)
1 dsp sugar
2 dsp cooking oil
$\frac{1}{2}$ tsp salt, to taste

REMPAH

2-3 red chillies, finely sliced
$\frac{1}{2}$ medium onion, chopped
3 cloves garlic, finely sliced
1 dsp blachan
4 candlenuts, crushed
3 dsp cooking oil

SERVES

4-6

PREPARATION

15 minutes

SAMBAL BINDI

Ladies fingers in dried prawn and sambal sauce

I love ladies fingers, cooked in any style or form. My mother used to steam them and make a tamarind dip with sambal blachan which I adore. Here is another recipe which often features in a Nonya home. It would complement a plain dish of fried fish (or prawns) in tamarind.
Photograph on page 29.

METHOD

1. Wash ladies fingers and top and tail. Slice diagonally $\frac{1}{2}$in apart.

2. Soak and drain dried prawns, reserving soaking liquid. Mince dried prawns in a food processor.

3. Make rempah by finely chopping ingredients in mini food processor. If using a liquidiser, add cooking oil or scant water to facilitate grinding.

4. Heat 2 dsp cooking oil in wok or saucepan and fry rempah until fragrant, stirring constantly to prevent burning.

5. Add dried or fresh prawns and stir to mix.

6. Add ladies fingers and stir to mix evenly with rempah. Cook for 3 minutes. Add some of the prawn soaking liquid if it is too dry.

7. Season with sugar and salt and simmer for a further 5 minutes.

8. Adjust seasoning and transfer to serving dish when cooked.

RICE

NASI TINDAY

NASI MINYAK

NASI LEMAK

NASI KUNYIT

NASI GORENG

TOMATO RICE

HAINANESE CHICKEN RICE

TO COOK PLAIN STEAMED RICE

Cooking rice takes some practice and you shouldn't be too upset if you didn't succeed at the first attempt. In Southeast Asia, it is one of the first things that mothers teach their daughters as soon as they are old enough to help in the kitchen. Apart from the amount of water to use, the age and variety of the rice, the type of saucepan used and controlling the heat are all factors that have to be taken into account to make perfect rice. The general rule of thumb is 1 cup of water to every cup of rice plus 1/2 cup over. Thus

1 cup rice - $1\frac{1}{2}$ cups water
2 cups rice - $2\frac{1}{2}$ cups water
3 cups rice - $3\frac{1}{2}$ cups water
4 cups rice - $4\frac{1}{2}$ cups water

Another method my mother taught me is to use my first finger as a measure. Rest the tip of your first finger upright just above the level of the rice. The water level should reach up to the first line of the finger. This seems to work fairly well for me but I also wonder at the accuracy of this principle as the human body is not exactly standard.

Wash rice in cold water to remove excess starch through 2-3 rinses until the water runs clear. Use a heavy based saucepan with a tight fitting lid. Add 1 teaspoon of salt, to taste. Cook on high heat and bring to the boil. Cover with a tight fitting lid and reduce heat to minimum setting. Cook for 20 minutes without lifting lid. At the end of 20 minutes, check to see if rice is cooked then remove from heat and replace lid to allow the rice to steam and fluff out.

R I c E

As in all Asian countries, rice forms the staple diet in Southeast Asia and is eaten at practically every meal, breakfast, lunch and dinner, especially among the Chinese who could eat it on its own with just a seasoning of soya sauce and perhaps the odd bit of fish or egg. Rice flour is made into noodles, cakes and pastries.

There are three main categories of rice - long grain, short grain, and glutinous - and within each category, many more varieties have been and are being developed. Short grain and glutinous rice are very starchy and mainly used in sweets and puddings although the Thais do sometimes eat glutinous rice as part of the main meal. Long grain rice is the most popular and is more commonly served with savoury courses. It is generally referred to as patna rice and now comes from the USA.

More recently Thai fragrant rice, another variety of long grain rice, has reached western markets and is gaining popularity with its delicate fragrance. It is slightly more glutinous than patna rice with a longer grain.

Japanese fragrant rice is also faintly perfumed and difficult to tell apart from Thai fragrant rice. However, the grains are slightly shorter and rounder. Much more expensive than any of the other rice, it is favoured by the Japanese who scorn any variety grown outside Japan, especially when used for sushi. However, much of the so-called Japanese rice available here is grown in the United States.

In Southeast Asia, long grain rice comes mainly from Thailand and Indonesia and different grades are available, priced accordingly. As rice is the main staple, we tend to be very particular about the quality of rice we eat and we would buy from specific stockists for a reliable grade. To complicate matters, there is the question of young rice and old rice - the age difference would determine the amount of water required to cook it. Older rice requires more water to swell the grains.

Basmati rice, the queen of rice, is mainly grown in Pakistan. It has a beautiful aroma and its grains are long and thin. Containing the least amount of gluten, it remains separate when cooked and is therefore ideal for use in biryanis and pilaus. For the average family, the cost of Basmati rice make it prohibitive for eating on a daily basis. Some supermarket chains are now stocking a mixture of basmati and Canadian wild rice. The contrasting colours of black and white and the different textures makes this an interesting variation. Canadian wild rice is in fact not a variety of rice but is a wild aquatic grass that produces grains.

Glutinous rice resembles the Italian arborio variety but it is very starchy and sticky when cooked. It is used mainly for desserts, when it is flavoured with coconut milk and served with coconut custards. Glutinous rice eaten with mangoes is a popular Thai dessert. It is also made into rice wine and rice vinegar.

Black glutinous rice is a variety of glutinous rice with a purplish black hue. It is not, as one would think, artificially coloured. It has a beautiful fragrance when cooked as a porridge and served with thick coconut cream.
See recipe on page 117.

If cooking on electric hob, turn off heat altogether once the rice has started to boil, cover with tight-fitting lid and leave on the hotplate for 20 minutes. Check after cooking period and leave to steam in its own heat to fluff out the grains. Turn the heat back on to minimum setting to keep warm.

Do not stir the rice after it has been cooked. If insufficient water has been added and the rice is still grainy, drizzle small amounts of boiling water down the sides of the saucepan and replace the lid, allowing the water to get to the bottom, creating more steam to swell the grains gently. Adding too much water all at the same time only results in the bottom layers becoming stewed and soggy whilst the upper layers still remain grainy.

Brown unpolished rice requires more cooking time and attention. The heat should be turned off after the first 15 minutes. Rest for 15 minutes and resume for 15 minutes to complete cooking.

Rice cooks remarkably well in the microwave oven. Keep to the same water quantity and cover with a lid. Cook for 15-20 minutes on high setting. A custom-made rice cooker for microwaves makes this method of rice cooking an even simpler procedure. Cooks perfect rice without sticking or crust.

To reheat cold rice, cover with cling film and microwave for 3-5 minutes. This is the most convenient and effective method. Alternatively it could be steamed in a colander over boiling water.

INGREDIENTS

2 cups Thai fragrant rice (or glutinous rice)
$3^1/_2$ cups water
$^1/_2$ tsp salt
2 pandan leaves, forked and tied into a knot

SERVES

4-6

PREPARATION TIME

15 minutes

N A S I   T I N D A Y

This is compressed rice and can be served with Satay, Soto ayam or Lontong with Sayur lodeh. You will need to make this the day before to allow the rice to set.

METHOD

1. Wash rice through several rinses until the water runs clear, drain and put into a heavy based saucepan.

2. Add water, salt and pandan leaves and bring to the boil.

3. As soon as the water starts to bubble furiously, turn the heat down to minimum setting (or turn the heat off completely if using electric hob) and cover with tightfitting lid. Cook for 20 minutes until all the water has been absorbed. Remove pandan leaves.

4. Transfer the rice onto a plastic or metal bowl and press down with a table spoon or spatula. Place a tight fitting plate resting directly onto the rice and press down with a heavy object e.g. a large pot weighted down with water. Leave for at least 4 hours until the rice is completely cold.

5. Cut into cubes or 2in x 2in x $^1/_4$in squares and serve as required.

INGREDIENTS
4 cups basmati rice
4 tbsp ghee
1 cinnamon bark
12 cardamons, lightly crushed
1 small onion, finely chopped
1in ginger, finely chopped
3 cloves garlic, finely chopped
4 oz (110g) raisins
4 cups boiling water
14oz (450ml)tinned evaporated milk
1 dsp salt

GARNISH
Fried crispy shallot rings

SERVES
6-8

PREPARATION TIME
20 minutes

Nasi minyak
Ghee rice flavoured with cinnamon and cardamon

A richly flavoured rice served on festive occasions. Complements strong Nonya curries and best served with a pickle relish like Achar to cut through the grease.

METHOD
1. Rinse the rice through several times until the water runs clear. Set aside.

2. Put onions, garlic and ginger in a food processor and chop for 10 seconds without turning it into a fine pulp.

3. Heat ghee in a heavy saucepan and throw in cinnamon and cardamons.

4. Fry onion mixture in the ghee until fragrant and lightly browned.

5. Add the rice and raisins and top up with milk and water. Season with salt. Bring to the boil and as soon as it starts to bubble furiously, cover with a tight fitting lid and leave to steam on the lowest setting for 20 minutes.

6. Remove from heat and leave covered to allow the rice to swell in its own steam.

7. Loosen the rice just before serving and sprinkle with crispy fried shallot rings.

INGREDIENTS

4 cups long grain rice
14oz (450ml) tinned coconut milk
3 cups water
1 tsp salt
1 dsp sugar
1 dsp cooking oil
4 pandan leaves

SERVES

6-8

PREPARATION TIME

20 minutes

N A S I   L E M A K
Coconut flavoured rice

Serving nasi lemak with coconut based dishes enhances the flavour of these dishes but it is delicious eaten on its own. It also goes very well with sambal dishes such as Sambal udang and Sambal ikan.

It should be made with coconut milk extracted from freshly grated coconut but as this is such a chore, I have given you the recipe made with tinned coconut milk. Tinned coconut milk is better than powdered coconut in this instance because powdered coconut has a heavier powdery consistency. If you would like to stick to the authentic taste, use 1 fresh grated coconut and mix with 5 cups water to extract milk.

METHOD

1. Rinse the rice several times until the water runs clear. Drain.

2. Put into a heavy based saucepan and add tinned coconut milk, water, salt, sugar and cooking oil. The oil will help to keep the rice grains separate. Stir to mix evenly.

3. Run a fork through the pandan leaves to release the fragrant oils and tie a loose knot. Add to the rice.

4. Bring to the boil on high heat.

5. As soon as the water begins to boil, lower the heat to minimum setting, cover with a tight fitting lid and cook for 20 minutes until rice is cooked.

6. Remove from heat and let the rice steam in its own heat for a further 5 minutes.

INGREDIENTS

4 cups glutinous rice
14oz (450ml) tinned coconut
3 tsp turmeric powder
3 cups water
1 tsp salt
4 pandan leaves

SERVES

6-8

PREPARATION

10 minutes

NASI KUNYIT
Turmeric flavoured glutinous rice cooked in coconut milk

Brightly coloured with turmeric and richly flavoured with coconut milk as well as perfumed with pandan leaves, it is the sort of rice that the Malays would serve on festive occasions such as weddings and Hari Raya Puasa, the festival following Ramadan.

It should be made with freshly grated coconut to get the best flavour but you can get away with using tinned coconut milk.

METHOD

1. Rinse the rice several times until the water runs clear. Drain.

2. Put into a heavy based saucepan with a tight fitting lid and add tinned coconut milk, water, salt and turmeric powder. Stir to mix evenly.

3. Run a fork through the pandan leaves to release the essential oils and tie into a loose knot. Add to the rice.

4. Bring to the boil on high heat.

5. As soon as the water begins to boil, lower the heat to minimum setting, cover with a tight fitting lid and cook for 20 minutes until rice is cooked.

6. Remove from heat and let the rice steam in its own heat for a further 5 minutes.

INGREDIENTS

*4 cups cooked rice (made from 2 cups
grains and 2 cups water)*
8oz (225g) shrimps
4oz (110g) Kenyan beans, finely chopped
$\frac{1}{2}$ - 1 red chilli, finely sliced
2 eggs, scrambled
2 shallots, finely chopped
1 tbsp light soya sauce
$\frac{1}{2}$ tsp salt
pinch of ground white pepper
1 dsp fish sauce (optional)
3 dsp cooking oil

GARNISHES

Crispy fried shallot rings
1 red chilli, finely sliced
1 spring onion, finely sliced
shredded iceberg lettuce
chopped coriander leaves
*Any one or a combination of the above
garnishes can be used.*

SERVES

6-8

PREPARATION

20 minutes

N A S I   G O R E N G

Fried rice is one way of using up leftover rice and leftover meats like roast chicken, beef or pork. Chopped ham, salami and cooked prawns are also acceptable ingredients. You can add as little or as much as is available to make a fairly substantial meal in itself, or as a rice dish to go with other dishes. The grains should be dry or your fried rice could end up being a stodgy mess and this is why leftovers are best. Always scramble the eggs separately before adding to the fried rice. The recipe below is one that works best for me. I use kenyan beans because they retain their crunchiness and do not release too much moisture.

METHOD

1. Heat 2 dsp cooking oil in a wok or large saucepan and scramble 2 beaten eggs until cooked. Remove and set aside.

2. Heat another 3 dsp cooking oil in the same wok and lightly brown chopped onions.

3. Add Kenyan beans and cook for 2-3 minutes.

4. Add prawns and sliced chillies and stir well. Cook for a further minute before seasoning with salt, pepper, and light soya sauce.

5. Add rice and stir to mix evenly.

6. Add scrambled eggs and stir to mix. Adjust seasoning and serve onto large platter or individual plates, garnished with crispy fried onion rings, shredded iceberg lettuce and coriander leaves.

INGREDIENTS

4 cups basmati rice, washed and drained
2 tsp salt
2 slices fresh ginger
1 medium onion, finely chopped
1 clove garlic
2 tbsp ghee
1 tsp cumin seeds
1 tsp mustard seeds
4 dsp tamarind soaked in 1 cup boiling water
6 ripe tomatoes, skinned and chopped

GARNISH

Fried shallot rings

SERVES

6-8

PREPARATION

20 minutes

TOMATO RICE

A lightly spiced and colourful rice with the tart but fruity flavour of tamarind. Ideal for serving with fish curry or sambal.

METHOD

1. Cook rice with 2 tsp salt and 4 cups water. Bring to the boil.

2. Cover tightly with lid and cook for 20 minutes on lowest setting without opening lid. Remove from heat and leave to steam for a further 10 minutes to allow rice to fluff out. Rake with a fork to separate grains.

3. In a separate saucepan, heat ghee and fry mustard and cumin seeds till they pop. Add finely chopped onions, ginger and garlic and fry until the onions are browning at the edges.

4. Add thick tamarind juice and chopped tomatoes and bring to the boil.

5. Simmer for 15 minutes on medium heat, stirring occasionally to prevent burning the bottom.

6. When the sauce has reduced, add freshly cooked rice to the tomato mixture and stir to mix evenly. Cover saucepan and leave to absorb flavours for 5-10 minutes before serving.

7. Serve garnished with fried shallot rings. Delicious served with fish curry.

INGREDIENTS

2 cups rice, washed
2¹/₂ cups chicken stock
1 in ginger, cut into julienne strips
3 cloves garlic, thinly sliced
1 tsp salt
1 dsp light soya sauce
1 dsp sesame oil
2 stalks spring onions

SERVES

4

PREPARATION

15 minutes

HAINANESE CHICKEN RICE

This is a very popular rice dish introduced by the Hainanese from the tiny island of Hunan in South China. It is eaten with steamed chicken flavoured with sesame oil and light soya sauce but the Singaporean influence has added a chilli, ginger and garlic dip that has turned a seemingly plain and uninteresting dish into a national favourite.
The flavoured rice is also delicious served with other dishes, especially if you prefer to eat your rice flavoured rather than plain.

METHOD

1. Made in conjunction with Hainan Chicken, you could use the chicken stock used to boil the chicken. Otherwise, ask your friendly butcher for some chicken carcass, or use chicken wings to make stock.

2. Rinse rice in several changes of water and drain thoroughly. Put in a heavy saucepan and add chicken stock.

3. Season with sesame oil, light soya, salt and a dash of ground white pepper.

4. Add the spring onions, julienned ginger and garlic slices and bring to the boil.

5. Once the stock starts to boil, cover with a tight fitting lid and turn the heat down to minimum setting (or completely off if cooking over an electric hob) and cook for 20 minutes. Do not open the lid during this time.

6. Check to see that the rice is cooked after 20 minutes and replace lid. Turn off the heat and allow the grains to fluff out in its own steam for another 5-10 minutes.

Noodles

LAKSA LEMAK

MEE GORENG

CHAR KUAY TEOW

CHAR BEEHOON

MEE SIAM

GUBAK KUAY TEOW

HOKKIEN PRAWN MEE

The varieties of noodle to look out for are:

FRESH WHEAT FLOUR NOODLES
Wheat flour is combined with egg and spun into thin round strands resembling spaghettini. You will find these in the refrigerated section of oriental supermarkets packed in plastic bags containing neat round bundles of individual servings, liberally doused with flour to prevent them from sticking. They are also made into flattish, wide fettucini-style ribbons. They should be boiled in plenty of water to remove the coating starch before stirfrying or adding to soups. Left refrigerated, they should keep for at least a week.

'OIL NOODLES' ('MEE' in Southeast Asia) is the name given to the freshly made thick round noodles gleaming with oil. Added colouring lends a bright yellow hue. They are firmer in texture and can be stirfried straight away without being blanched. This is the variety used in the Singapore-Indian style noodle dish called Mee goreng. They are also added to soups as in the Hokkien prawn mee

DRIED WHEAT FLOUR NOODLES
Made of the same ingredients as the fresh wheat flour noodles, these are sold in plastic bags in various thickness in nestlike swirls. Use the first grade thickness as a substitute for the oil noodles above. They will need to be boiled in plenty of water to soften and well drained before stirfrying or adding to soups.

FRESH HO FUN (Rice Flour Noodles)
Made from rice flour, hofun are flat tagliatelli-

NOODLES

One of the most valuable products that the Chinese brought with them to Southeast Asia must be the noodle. The first noodle was invented in China around the first century. Noodles have not only become popular but are second only to rice, and feature regulaly in their diet. They were also introduced by the Chinese to countries like Korea, Japan, Taiwan, IndoChina and Southeast Asia who created their own styles of cooking and serving noodles. They are very versatile and combined with soups, vegetables and a few slivers of meat or seafood, make filling one-dish meals. They are most appropriately served at luncheon parties as a little meat goes a long way, but they can be made more substantial with generous portions of seafood or meats or perhaps another starter dish.

Commonly made from rice or wheat flour, they can also be made from mung bean starch and buckwheat. This is one product that is mostly factory made, rarely made at home, as commercial noodlemaking is an ancient Chinese craft better left to the experts. Noodles are sold in dried form or fresh and cooked in a variety of methods:
stirfried, panfried (Cantonese style of blanching in boiling water, drained and fried to a crisp in a smouldering hot wok, and served with a sauce with meats and thickened with cornstarch), served in soups or simply boiled and served with a sauce. The Nonyas took every opportunity of conjuring a variety of hot sauces to accompany these noodles and several dishes have become firm favourites with every nationality residing in Southeast Asia.

style ribbon noodles originating from Guandong province. They are also well oiled to separate the strands. They do not need blanching before cooking and are therefore suitable for stirfrying.

DRIED HO FUN are available in two varieties. Those made in Vietnam are opaque and compact whilst those made in Thailand tend to be voluminous and have a transparent and flimsy quality. The Vietnamese version has a firmer texture. Both need to be boiled in plenty of water to soften and drained before use. If they are to be stirfried, it is recommended that they are left to dry out so that they stay crisp or excess water will make your dish soggy.

RICE VERMICELLI

These thin white wiry strands of dried noodles should not be boiled before use. Instead they should be soaked in fairly warm water to soften for about 5 minutes and well drained. Those made in Singapore have added cornstarch which gives them a firmer texture when cooked. They are not sold fresh.

TUNG HOON NOODLES (TRANSPARENT OR GLASS NOODLES)

Made from the starch of the mung bean flour, they are like clear glass strands and are tough and wiry in their dried form. Buy them in smaller 2 oz packs rather than the economy size as they are difficult to separate unless you resort to the use of secateurs. They soften almost immediately upon contact with hot water and should be left to soak for only a few minutes and well drained. They are popularly served in soups or made into salads especially in Thai recipes.

INGREDIENTS

8oz (225g) rice vermicelli noodles, soaked in hot water to soften and drained

6oz (175g) fresh beansprouts, blanched for 2 minutes and drained

8oz (225g) coconut powder mixed with 1 pint (570ml) hot water

4oz (110g) dried prawns, soaked in 1 cup boiling water for 30 minutes

8oz (225g) fish cakes, deep fried for 5 minutes, finely sliced

2 tsp salt, to taste

1lb (450g) fresh seawater prawns, (size 21-25)

1 cup mint leaves (as substitute for Daun Kesom)

1/4 cucumber, peeled and deseeded, and cut into thin julienne strips

2 pints (1.2 litres) prawn stock or water

REMPAH

8 stalks lemon grass, finely sliced
2in galanggal
10 candlenuts
4 red chillies
1in fresh turmeric or 1 tsp powder
1 large onion, finely chopped
4 cloves garlic, finely chopped
1 dsp blachan
4 dsp cooking oil

GARNISH

Cucumber cut into julienne strips
Fresh mint leaves

SERVES

4-6

PREPARATION

30 minutes

LAKSA LEMAK
Nonya noodles in spicy coconut sauce

METHOD

1. Make rempah in liquidiser.

2. Drain soaked dried prawns and chop in food processor for 10 seconds.

3. Deep fry fish cakes and beancurd. Slice thinly and set aside.

4. Cook tiger prawns in their shell in 1 pint water for 5 minutes until they turn pink. Remove from saucepan with a slotted spoon and set aside, reserving the cooking water for stock.

5. When prawns are cold enough to handle, remove central vein and cut into half along the length and set aside.

6. Heat 2 dsp cooking oil in deep saucepan. Fry rempah until fragrant and add minced dried prawns. Stir for a few seconds. Add stock or water and the reserved prawn stock and bring to the boil. Simmer for 30 minutes.

7. Add coconut milk and season with salt. Lower heat and simmer for 5 minutes. Keep hot.

TO ASSEMBLE

8. In a second large saucepan, bring 4 pints (2.25 litres) of water to the boil and blanch soaked noodles and beansprouts for 5-10 seconds to re-heat (use a Chinese wire sieve custom-made for this purpose if you have one). Alternatively, place noodles and beansprouts in serving bowl and warm in microwave for 10 seconds.

9. Arrange a few cooked prawns, fish cakes and fried beancurd on top of the warmed noodles.

10. Pour 2-3 ladles of hot coconut sauce onto the noodles and serve garnished with julienned cucumbers and fresh mint leaves.

This dish requires elaborate preparations but the sensational flavour is always highly lauded. It is best served as a luncheon dish. As it is very filling and rich you can get away with just the one dish. By being generous with the prawns and fish cakes, it becomes a meal in itself.

INGREDIENTS

8oz (225g) egg noodles (boiled for 5 minutes to soften and drained)
4oz (110g) beansprouts (rinsed and drained)
2 eggs (scrambled) and set aside
2 squares of beancurd, deep fried to a crisp and cut into slices
2 tsp crushed dried chillies mixed with 1 tbsp boiling water to make a paste
2 cloves garlic, finely chopped
1 small onion, finely chopped
4oz (110g) lean lamb steak, finely sliced
4 tbsp cooking oil
2-3oz (50g) Chinese Greens (choi sum)
1 tsp dark soya sauce
$^1/_2$ tsp salt, to taste
1 dsp tomato ketchup
2 stalks spring onion, cut into 1$^1/_2$in lengths

GARNISHES

4 oriental limes or 1 lemon cut into 4 wedges
a sprig of Chinese or European celery leaves
1 red chilli, sliced
1 green chilli, sliced

SERVES

Serves 4-6

PREPARATION

20 minutes

MEE GORENG
Indian hawker-style egg noodles stirfried with lamb slices

This noodle dish is a curious mixture of Indian and Chinese styles. Sold normally by Indian vendors who have no history of serving noodles, except of course in Southeast Asia, it uses Chinese ingredients of beancurd, beansprouts and soya sauce. The use of hot chilli paste is not in keeping with Chinese cooking style but then again, the people of Southeast Asia are so fond of incendiary dishes that they have the tendency to spice everything up. Lamb was originally probably used because the Indians, most of whom are Hindus or Muslims, do not eat beef or pork. You could use beef slices if preferred, breast of chicken or even prawns. Try and keep the heat as high as possible as this is a fairly dry dish with a slightly charred flavour.

METHOD

1. Heat oil in wok or deep saucepan until smoking, and lightly brown chopped onions and garlic.

2. Add lamb slices and stir fry till they have turned colour. Cook for a further minute, stirring all the time.

3. Add chilli paste, soya sauce and tomato ketchup and season with salt to taste.

4. Add noodles, greens and beansprouts and mix well. Cook for a further 2 minutes.

5. Stir in scrambled eggs and spring onions and fried beancurd pieces and mix well.

6. Cook for a minute and transfer onto serving platter, garnished with freshly sliced green and red chillies, Chinese celery leaves and lemon wedges.

7. A squeeze of lemon juice complements the flavours.

INGREDIENTS

8oz (225g) fresh broad rice noodles (HoFun)
If using dried HoFun from the packet, cook in salted boiling water for 8-10 minutes until softened. Rinse under cold running water to remove excess starch and drain well. Leave for at least 20 minutes.

4oz (110g) beansprouts, rinsed and drained over colander
4oz (110g) fish cakes, thinly sliced
4oz (110g) cooked peeled prawns
1 Chinese sausage, thinly sliced
3 cloves garlic, finely chopped
2 eggs, scrambled
$\frac{1}{2}$ tsp salt, to taste
2oz (50g) Chinese greens (choi sum)
2 stalks spring onions, cut into $1\frac{1}{2}$in lengths
2 tbsp cooking oil
2 tsp crushed dried chillies mixed with 1 tbsp boiling water to make a paste
1 dsp thick soya
1 dsp sugar

SERVES

4-6

PREPARATION

20 minutes

CHAR KUAY TEOW

Broad rice noodles stirfried with Chinese sausage, fish cakes, prawns and egg

When Europeans refer to Singapore noodles, I guess they must mean this dish because it is definitely one of Singapore's all-time favourites. The street vendor usually has a variety of noodles which he can cook to this particular style - rice vermicelli, egg noodles, and broad rice noodles (Kuay teow in the Hokkien dialect or Hofun according to the Cantonese dialect).
Stirfried in a giant commercial wok over an intense turbo gas flame, the noodles have a dry and slightly charred flavour. The vendor has all his ingredients ready which he throws in one after another in an ordered sequence and within 2-3 minutes they are done. Cooked at home, this takes a little longer because the intensity of the heat in the domestic cooker is much lower. However, the actual cooking time is 8-10 minutes and the dish should be eaten straight from the pan to be at its best.
Photograph on page 61.

METHOD

1. Heat oil in wok until smoking and lightly brown chopped garlic.

2. Working with speed, add fish cakes, Chinese sausage, prawns and Chinese greens and stir for a minute.

3. Add seasonings - chilli sauce, thick soya sauce, sugar and salt, to taste.

4. Add noodles and mix evenly. Cook for a minute.

5. Add beansprouts and spring onions, stirring well.

6. Add scrambled eggs and stir.

7. Transfer onto serving dish.

INGREDIENTS

6 shallots, thinly sliced
2 cloves garlic, thinly sliced (optional)
2 tbsp cooking oil
8oz (225g) rice vermicelli noodles, soaked in warm-water for 10 minutes and well drained
8oz (225g) fresh beansprouts, rinsed in cold water and well drained
8oz (225g) choi sum (Chinese greens) or any crisp green vegetable like broccoli or mange-tout

SAUCES AND SEASONINGS

2 dsp fish sauce
2 dsp light soya sauce
salt and pepper to taste
1 dsp sugar

SUGGESTED MEATS

Any of the following meats can be used to flavour the noodles or a combination of all of them for variety:
8oz (225g) cooked peeled prawns (or green prawns)
8oz (225g) cooked pork or chicken (leftover roast chicken or pork) Otherwise, boil pork steaks or chicken breast with 3 slices of ginger in 4 cups of water until cooked, leave to cool and slice into thin strips. Reserve any leftover liquid.
8oz (225g) fresh squid, cleaned and cut into rings
8oz (225g) fish cakes (available from Chinese supermarkets)

SERVES

4-6

PREPARATION

20 minutes

C H A R   b e e h o o N

Singapore vermicelli noodles

The meat content in this dish can be varied according to personal likes and dislikes and availability of ingredients. A variety of meats can also be combined in any desired quantity. The ratio of meat to noodles will depend on whether the dish is intended to be a main course or a filler.

METHOD

Noodles are best stirfried in a wok but a very large deep saucepan would also do the trick.

1. Heat oil and lightly brown shallots and garlic.

2. Add raw meats if used (squid, fish cakes or prawns), stirring continuously to prevent sticking. Prawns should turn pink and squid lose their transparent look when they are cooked.

3. Add sauces and seasonings, followed by Chinese greens or chosen vegetables.

4. Add beansprouts and stirfry for a further minute.

5. Add blanched noodles and mix well. Avoid adding any more liquid if a fairly dry noodle dish is desired but if the heat is too intense and the noodles are sticking to the pot, sprinkle with leftover pork or chicken stock or water.

6. Adjust seasoning by adding fish sauce or light soya at this stage as it is more easily absorbed than salt granules as well as providing more flavour.

7. Transfer onto large platter or serving dish and garnish with fried onion rings, shredded lettuce or coriander leaves. A side dish of freshly sliced chillies sprinkled with light soya sauce can be served with it.

INGREDIENTS

16oz (450g) pkt rice vermicelli noodles, soaked
to soften and well drained
16oz (450g) fresh beansprouts
2oz (50g) Chinese chives, finely snipped (use
English chives if unavailable)
2 beancurd cakes, deep fried and diced
6 hardboiled eggs, sliced
16oz (450g) green prawns, peeled
1 tsp salt
8 oriental limes, or 1 lemon cut into 8 wedges

4 tbsp cooking oil
2 pints (1 litre) water
4 dsp tamarind juice, soaked in 2 cups boiling
water to extract juice
2 tbsp tauceo (yellow beans) mashed with a fork
3 tbsp sugar
1 dsp salt

REMPAH
20 dried chillies
1 large onion, finely chopped
4 cloves garlic, finely chopped
10 candlenuts
1 dsp blachan
3 tbsp cooking oil

SERVES
8-10

PREPARATION
45 minutes

MEE SIAM
Spicy vermicelli noodles with tamarind

The name implies that the recipe was borrowed from Thailand. It certainly has the spicy hot, sweet and sour elements that are the hallmarks of Thai cuisine. Believe it or not, this is my favourite breakfast dish. Southeast Asians are fond of savoury dishes for the first meal in the day and a meal-in-one dish like noodles is ideal as they are easy and quick to eat. The strong flavours in this particular dish would definitely wake you up and get all systems going.

As it is unlikely that the European palate will adapt to such strong flavours for breakfast, it might be more appropriate for lunch. The elaborate preparation it entails makes it pointless to make small quantities, so cook for a party.

METHOD

1. Snip dried chillies with kitchen scissors into $\frac{1}{2}$in lengths to facilitate grinding. Remove stalks. Soak in 1 cup boiling water for 20 minutes to soften. Strain, discarding the seeds that settle to the bottom.

2. Make rempah in liquidiser, using scant water to facilitate blending. Divide rempah into 2 equal portions.

3. Heat 2 dsp cooking oil and fry half the rempah for a few minutes until fragrant, stirring the bottom constantly to prevent burning and sticking.

4. Add tauceo (yellow beans), minced dried prawns and sugar. Stir for 2 minutes.

5. Top up with 2 pints water and tamarind juice and bring to the boil. Season with salt and simmer on medium heat for 20 minutes. Keep hot on low heat.

TO COOK NOODLES

6. Heat 2 tbsp cooking oil in wok and fry the remaining half of rempah until fragrant. Add sugar and salt.

7. Add peeled prawns and stir to mix evenly until prawns turn pink.

8. Add beansprouts and sprinkle with salt and mix well. Cook for 2 minutes.

9. Add noodles and stir to mix until noodles are evenly coated with rempah.

10. Cook for 2-3 minutes and keep warm.

TO ASSEMBLE

Put a helping of noodles on a deep soup or pasta dish and garnish with sliced hard boiled eggs, diced deep fried beancurd cakes and chopped chives. Pour 2 ladles of steaming hot tamarind sauce on top and serve immediately.
A squeeze of lime juice accentuates the tamarind flavour.

INGREDIENTS

2lb (900g) shin of beef or brisket
1lb (450g) beef tripe, cleaned
4 pints (2.5 litres) water
1 in galanggal, bruised
2 tsp salt
1 dsp sugar
1 tsp black peppercorns
1 tbsp dark soya
2 stalks Chinese celery or use Continental celery

1 lb (450g) Ho Fun
8 oz (225g) beansprouts, blanched
1 tbsp chopped coriander leaves
1-2 fresh red chillies

GARNISHES

fried onion rings

SERVES

4-6

PREPARATION

20 minutes

GUBAK KUAY TEOW

Broad rice noodles in beef stock with tripe

My father who doesn't eat pork would always opt for this noodle dish when we visited the stalls for a bite to eat. Eating out in stalls in Singapore is inexpensive and the quality of food so good that you never need an excuse to eat out. This is a meal in itself and ideal for a family luncheon. You could use the carcass from your rib of roast beef to make the stock. Omit tripe if you are not keen on offal.

METHOD

1. Make beef stock by boiling tripe, beef bones (if available) and brisket, skimming the scum until the soup runs clear.

2. Season with celery, galanggal, peppercorns, soya sauce, salt and sugar.

3. Simmer on medium heat for $1\frac{1}{2}$ hours until the tripe and meat are tender. Remove meats and leave to cool but keep the stock simmering on low heat.

4. Finely slice tripe and beef into bitesized pieces. Set aside.

TO ASSEMBLE
1. In a separate pot, bring 2 pints of water to the boil and use a Chinese noodle sieve to blanch individual servings of noodles and a handful of beansprouts for a minute. Drain and place in serving bowl.

2. Sprinkle sliced tripe and beef over the top of the noodles, garnish with chopped coriander leaves and fried onion rings and pour 2 ladles of hot beef stock over it.

3. Repeat for each serving.

Serve with fresh chilli slices.

INGREDIENTS

2lbs (900g) green prawns
(size 21-25)
1lb (450g) yellow 'oil' noodles
8oz (225g) beansprouts
6oz (175g) kangkong (water convolvulus)
4 pints (2.5 litres) water
1 dsp sugar
1 dsp salt
1 dsp dark soya sauce
2 dsp light soya sauce
1 tbsp fish sauce
$\frac{1}{2}$ tsp ground white pepper
1lb (450g) pork ribs

GARNISHES

1 tbsp fried onion rings
12 fresh red chillies, finely sliced
2 tbsp light soya sauce

SERVES

6-8

PREPARATION

30 minutes

HOKKIEN PRAWN meE

The Chinese immigrants from Fukien in south China brought with them this simple yet delicious noodle soup dish made famous by the hawker stalls of Singapore. A meal in itself, it is ideally served as a luncheon dish. It is important to get a rich stock by boiling prawn shells and pork bones.

METHOD

1. Shell the prawns and dry roast the shells in a wok or saucepan until they are crisp and brown.

2. Bring water to the boil and add pork ribs and roasted prawn shells. Simmer for 45 minutes to obtain a good stock, skimming off the scum as they rise to the surface.

3. Plunge the peeled prawns in the stock for 5 minutes until they are curled and turned a deep pink. Remove and set aside.

4. Remove bones and prawn shells and put through a strainer into another pot. Keep the stock on simmering point and season with salt, sugar, sauces and ground white pepper.

5. In a separate pot, bring water to the boil and using a Chinese blanching sieve, blanch individual servings of noodles, beansprouts and kangkong for 2-3 minutes. Place into a deep serving bowl. Alternatively, blanch noodles, beansprouts and kangkong separately and divide into individual serving bowls.

6. Put cooked prawns on top of the noodles and pour 2 ladles of boiling hot pork and prawn stock over them. Garnish with crispy fried shallot rings and serve with a side dish of freshly sliced chillies in light soya sauce.

FISH AND SEAFOOD

CHILLI CRAB

IKAN TAUCEO

IKAN PLACHIAN

UDANG MASAK NANAS

IKAN SENTAL

IKAN MASAK ASSAM PEKAT

SAMBAL UDANG

UDANG GORENG ASSAM

SAMBAL IKAN BILIS

IKAN BILIS TEMPRA

MALABAR FISH CURRY

ACHAR IKAN

OTAK OTAK

CHILLI CRAB

INGREDIENTS

2-3 large crabs (or use 2lb [900g] Atlantic crab claws)

2-4 red chillies, thinly sliced
3 cloves garlic, finely sliced
1 medium onion, finely sliced
1 in ginger, finely sliced
4 dsp cooking oil

2 dsp brown sugar
2 tbsp tomato ketchup
1 dsp yellow bean paste (tauceo) (optional)
$\frac{1}{2}$ tsp salt, to taste
1 egg, beaten (optional)
1 dsp brandy
1 cup water

GARNISH
Fresh coriander leaves
Spring onion curls

SERVES
4-6

PREPARATION
20 minutes

METHOD

1. Clean and chop crabs into smaller pieces. Bash shells lightly with a hammer to allow sauce to penetrate.

2. Roughly chop onions, ginger, garlic and chillies in a food processor for 10 seconds.

3. Heat 3 dsp cooking oil in a wok or large saucepan and fry onion mixture until almost brown and fragrant, stirring constantly to prevent burning.

4. Add tauceo, tomato ketchup, water and season with salt and sugar. Add 1 dsp brandy.

5. Cook for 5 minutes under medium heat, stirring to prevent sticking at the bottom.

6. Add crab, stirring to coat evenly, cover with lid and simmer for 10 minutes.

7. Add beaten egg if desired to thicken sauce just before serving, stirring to disperse the egg.

8. Serve garnished with fresh coriander leaves or spring onion curls.

This is probably one of the signature dishes of Singapore, originally made popular by the east coast stalls specialising in seafood and crabs. Best cooked in its shell, crab is of course to be eaten in casual mode, with a bib, using your fingers to crack open the shell and sucking out the meat and the delicious sauce. Be warned, you could end up with burning lips but the experience is delightful all the same.

At the Singapura Restaurant where the clientele and the pace are somewhat faster, I have used Atlantic crab claws which are so much easier to eat while preserving one's dignity. They are also available all the year round.

Another variation which has worked very well is to replace crab with tiger prawns.

INGREDIENTS

1lb (450g) fish fillet (dusted with cornflour and deep fried)
oil for deep frying

1 small onion finely sliced
2 cloves garlic, finely sliced
1 in ginger, julienned
1 fresh red chilli, finely sliced

2 dsp tauceo
1 dsp dark soya sauce
1 dsp fish sauce
1 dsp vinegar
1 dsp brown sugar
pinch of salt to taste
dash of ground white pepper
2 dsp cooking oil
$\frac{1}{2}$ cup water

SERVES

4

PREPARATION

15 minutes

IKAN TAUCEO

Fish cooked in yellow bean sauce.

Recommended fish: halibut steaks, salmon, grey mullet, cod and haddock steaks, trout, plaice, lemon or Dover sole, brill)

METHOD

1. Heat cooking oil in a small saucepan and lightly brown sliced onions and garlic and ginger.

2. Add tauceo, sugar, dark soya, fish sauce, vinegar and salt to taste .

3. Add water and bring to the boil. Simmer for 5 minutes and add red chillies.

4. Set aside and reheat just before serving.

5. Deep fry fish until cooked and crispy.

6. Drain on paper towel and place on deep serving dish.

7. Pour reheated sauce over the top.

If you prefer not to fry your fish, add raw fish omitting the cornflour into the sauce after stage 3 and cook for a further 5-10 minutes, depending on the thickness of the fish.

INGREDIENTS

1lb (450g) fillet of fish, dusted with cornflour and deep fried
oil for deep frying

1 small onion, finely sliced
2 cloves garlic, finely sliced
1in ginger, julienned
1 fresh red chilli, finely sliced
1 tomato, quartered
1 dsp tamarind, soaked in 1 cup boiling water to extract juice (substitute: 1 dsp vinegar or 2 dsp lemon juice)
8oz (225g) pineapple pieces and juice, tinned or fresh
2 dsp cooking oil

1 dsp cooking oil
1 dsp fish sauce
1 dsp palm sugar (substitute dark brown sugar)
1 dsp sherry (optional)
pinch of salt to taste
dash of ground white pepper

GARNISH
Fresh coriander leaves or
Spring onion curls

SERVES
4

PREPARATION
20 minutes

IKAN PLACHIAN

Fish with pineapple and ginger sauce.
Recommended fish: brill or halibut steaks, salmon, grey mullet, cod and haddock steaks, lemon or Dover sole, sword fish or any of the exotic Indian Ocean fish.

METHOD

1. Heat cooking oil in a small saucepan and lightly brown sliced onions, garlic and ginger.

2. Add tamarind juice, dark soya, fish sauce, pineapple pieces and juice from the can, palm sugar, sherry (if used) and salt to taste.

3. Bring to the boil and simmer for 5 minutes and add red chillies and tomatoes.

4. Set aside and re-heat just before serving.

5. Deepfry fish until cooked and crispy.

6. Drain on kitchen paper and place on deep serving dish.

7. Pour reheated sauce over the fish and garnish with spring onions or coriander leaves.

INGREDIENTS

12 large mediterranean prawns or
Size 8-12 tiger prawns
16oz (450g) canned pineapple pieces and juice
or use a fresh pineapple
4 tbsp tamarind soaked in 2 cups boiling water to
extract juice
2 pints (1 litre) water
1 tsp salt to taste
2-3 dsp sugar to taste
2 stalks lemon grass, trimmed and lightly bruised
few sprigs of fresh basil leaves
1 fresh red chilli, halved

REMPAH
2 stalks lemon grass, finely sliced
$^1/_2$ in galanggal
1 in turmeric
6 candlenuts
1 dsp blachan
4 red chillies, finely sliced
1 medium onion, finely chopped

GARNISH
Fresh basil leaves

SERVES

4-6

PREPARATION

20 minutes

U d a n G   M a s a K   N a n a S

Mediterranean or large sized tiger prawns in their shells cooked in a tamarind sauce with pineapples, flavoured with lemon grass.

Firm fleshed fish such as halibut, monkfish, skate or pomfret can also be substituted for prawns.

METHOD

1. Make rempah in a blender with 1 cup of water. In this recipe, it does not matter if the rempah is watery as it will not be fried.

2. Put 1 litre water, rempah, tamarind juice, sugar, pineapples, crushed lemon grass, fresh chilli and salt in a deep saucepan.

3. Bring to the boil and simmer for 10 minutes.

4. Add prawns or fish and cook for 10 minutes until cooked.

5. Adjust seasoning.

6. Serve in a deep bowl and garnish with a few fresh basil leaves.

This is my favourite Nonya dish. The sweet, hot and sour flavours are enhanced to the fullest in this dish whilst the sweet juices of the prawns are retained in their shells. The thin sauce is somewhat like a hot and sour soup, which I usually find myself drinking spoonfuls of, although it is really meant to be ladled onto plain steamed rice.

INGREDIENTS
4 mackerel (gutted)
$^1/_2$ tsp salt
cooking oil for shallow frying

STUFFING
4 fresh red chillies or 10 dried chillies
3 cloves garlic
8 candlenuts (or use 2oz ground almonds)
4 slices galanggal
$^1/_2$in fresh turmeric or use $^1/_2$ tsp powder
$^1/_2$ tsp salt
juice of $^1/_2$ lemon
3 tbsp cooking oil

SERVES
4-6

PREPARATION
20 minutes

IKAN SENTAL
Spicy stuffed mackerel

Being an oily fish, mackerel is best cooked grilled or fried to a crisp. The lightly spiced stuffing brings out the best in this fish.
Photograph on page 43.

METHOD
1. Make 3 diagonal slits along the side of the fish. Rub with salt.

2. Chop the stuffing rempah in a mini food processor to get a coarse paste.

3. Fry the stuffing mix in small saucepan for 5 minutes.

4. Put stuffing into the slits and the stomach cavity of the fish.

5. Heat cooking oil in a frying pan or wok and shallow fry fish on medium heat until cooked through, turning the fish carefully with a slotted spoon to cook evenly and prevent burning. (Alternatively, grill on medium heat 5-10 minutes on either side.)

6. Drain on kitchen paper and serve immediately or keep warm in oven.

INGREDIENTS

1lb (450g) firm-fleshed fish such as halibut
steaks, skate, monkfish
4 tbsp tamarind soaked in 2 cups boiling water to
extract juice
3 tbsp cooking oil
2 dsp sugar
1 tsp salt
2 tomatoes, quartered
2 stalks lemon grass, trimmed and lightly bruised

REMPAH

6 large red chillies
1 medium onion
4 candlenuts
1in fresh turmeric or 1 tsp ground turmeric
1 dsp blachan

GARNISH

Fresh sprigs of parsley, mint or basil

SERVES

4

PREPARATION

20 minutes

IKAN MASAK ASSAM PEKAT

Skate cooked in chilli and tamarind sauce flavoured with lemon grass
This is not a mild dish but once your tastebuds have got used to coping with
chillies (with practice), you will love the flavour of this rempah and appreciate
how it can complement fish in the best possible way.

METHOD

1. Make rempah by liquidising in blender with 3 tbsp cooking oil
and some of the tamarind juice to facilitate blending.

2. Heat remaining cooking oil in large deep saucepan and fry
rempah till fragrant. Add remaining tamarind juice.

3. Bring to the boil and simmer for 5 minutes, then add remaining
ingredients.

4. Cook for a further 5 minutes to reduce the sauce slightly before
adding fish which should be cooked for only 5-10 minutes depending on the thickness and type of fish used.

5. Serve garnished with sprig of parsley, mint or basil leaves for
colour.

INGREDIENTS

2lb (900g) fresh seawater prawns (size 21-25 is ideal), peel and de-vein
2 dsp cooking oil
1 tbsp brown sugar
1 dsp tamarind soaked in 1 cup boiling water to extract juice
$^1/_2$ tsp salt, to taste

REMPAH

1 medium red onion or 10 oriental shallots
1 dsp blachan
6 candlenuts
10 dried red chillies or 1 dsp chilli powder
$^1/_2$in galanggal
3 dsp cooking oil

SERVES

4-6

PREPARATION

20 minutes

S A M B A L   U D A N G

Tiger prawns cooked in a hot and spicy sauce flavoured with blachan.

This is a popular dish among Malays and Nonyas. Judging from the number of orders for this dish at the Singapura restaurants in London, its popularity has reached western palates.

Sambal udang goes particularly well with Nasi lemak (coconut rice) and fresh cucumber. If you cannot get hold of green seawater prawns, use cooked peeled prawns but cook only for a minute to heat through.

METHOD

1. Grind rempah finely in mini food processor, adding a little of the tamarind juice to facilitate blending.

2. Heat 2 dsp cooking oil and fry rempah until fragrant. Add tamarind juice, salt and sugar to taste. Bring to the boil.

3. Simmer for 5 minutes and add prawns. Cook for 5 minutes until prawns have turned pink and are cooked through.

UDANG GORENG ASSAM

Shallow fried tiger prawns in their shells marinated with tamarind.

This used to be a favourite dish in the family and there was never enough to go round, partly because of the size of my family but mainly because it is so moreish. Terribly easy to make and guaranteed to please.
In the summer when you are having a barbecue, the prawns can be threaded onto skewers and grilled over charcoal instead of fried.

INGREDIENTS
12 large size tiger prawns (Size 8-12) in their shells
2 tbsp tamarind soaked in 1/2 cup boiling water for 20 minutes
1 tsp salt
1 tsp brown sugar
1 cup cooking oil for shallow frying

GARNISH
Diced cucumber
Shredded iceberg lettuce
Fresh parsley

SERVES
6
Allow at least 2 prawns per person

PREPARATION
10 minutes

METHOD
1. Make a slit across the top of the prawn and remove the black vein. Trim off the legs if desired. Rinse and pat dry with a paper towel.

2. When the soaked tamarind has cooled sufficiently to be handled, mash with fingers to separate the pulp from the seed.

3. Marinate the prawns with the tamarind mixture and season with salt and sugar. Leave to marinate for at least 30 minutes.

4. Heat cooking oil in frying pan. Remove prawns from marinade and fry for 5 minutes, turning the prawns over to cook evenly on either side.

5. Remove from the cooking oil with a slotted spoon and serve on a bed of sliced cucumbers or shredded iceberg lettuce. Garnish with a sprig of parsley.

INGREDIENTS
1lb (450g) ikan bilis
1 cup oil for shallow frying
2 dsp sugar
$^1/_2$ tsp salt, to taste
1 tbsp tamarind, soaked in 1 cup boiling water to extract juice

REMPAH
3 cloves garlic
1 medium red onion (or 10 oriental shallots)
1 dsp blachan
5 candlenuts
10 dried chillies or 1 dsp chilli powder
3 dsp cooking oil

SERVES
4-6

PREPARATION
20 minutes

SAMBAL IKAN BILIS
Crispy fried anchovies in hot sambal sauce.

Southeast Asians always keep a cache of ikan bilis in the refrigerator or larder ready gutted and cleaned for use - it comes in handy when you have unexpected guests and need to rustle something up.
They are also often shallow fried and served along with peanuts and prawn crackers as snacks with Tiger beer. They go particularly well with coconut rice (Nasi lemak) and fresh cucumber.

Remove the heads of the larger varieties. Then, between your thumb and forefinger, gently squeeze the body of the anchovy on either side. This will split the fish into two and allow you to remove the skeleton easily. However, the fish bones when fried to a crisp are quite edible. On no account wash the fish if you want them to remain crispy after frying.

METHOD
1. Make rempah by blending finely in mini food processor. If using liquidiser, add scant water to facilitate grinding.

2. Heat 2 dsp cooking oil in wok or saucepan and fry rempah until fragrant, stirring constantly to prevent sticking and burning.

3. Add tamarind juice, sugar, and salt to taste.

4. Simmer on gentle heat for 5 minutes. Keep hot and set aside.

5. Shallow fry ikan bilis in 1 cup cooking oil until golden brown and crispy.

6. Remove with a slotted spoon and dry on paper towel. Add to sambal sauce, mix and serve.

INGREDIENTS

1lb (450g) ikan bilis, cleaned
8oz (225g) raw peanuts in their skin or use
roasted peanuts
$^1/_2$in galanggal, thinly sliced
1 medium onion, thinly sliced
1 red chilli, finely sliced
2 cloves garlic, thinly sliced
1 tbsp brown sugar
1 tbsp tamarind, soaked in 1 cup boiling water to
soften and extract juice
$^1/_2$ tsp salt, to taste
3 dsp cooking oil
1 cup oil for shallow frying

SERVES

4-6

PREPARATION

15 minutes

I K A N   B I L I S
T E M P R A

Ikan Bilis and Peanut in galanggal and tamarind sauce.
Here is another recipe for ikan bilis which I think you will love. It has a fragrant sweet and sour flavour with just a touch of pungency and is delicious served with plain steamed rice.

METHOD

1. Shallow fry raw peanuts in 1 cup cooking oil until cooked (5 minutes). Remove from oil and drain on kitchen paper. Set aside.

2. In the same oil, shallow fry ikan bilis until brown and crispy. Remove from oil and drain on kitchen paper. Set aside. Discard oil.

3. Heat 3 dsp fresh cooking oil in wok or large saucepan and lightly brown sliced onions, galanggal and garlic.

4. Add chillies, tamarind juice, sugar and salt to taste. Simmer for 5 minutes on gentle heat and keep hot.

5. When ready to serve, combine fried ikan bilis, nuts and sauce and stir to mix evenly. The fish and nuts lose their crispiness if the sauce is added too early.

INGREDIENTS

2lb fish (900g) (e.g. mackerel, cod steaks, tuna steaks, monkfish tails)
1in ginger, 1 medium red onion, 2 cloves of garlic
6 tbsp tamarind water
1 cup water
$\frac{1}{2}$ fresh coconut or 2oz (50g) coconut powder, mixed with $\frac{1}{2}$ pint (275ml) of water
1 large aubergine or 3-4 baby aubergines or 8oz (225g) ladies fingers
6 tbsp cooking oil
1 teaspoon mustard seed
1 tbsp curry leaves
1 piece of cinnamon stick
3 tomatoes, quartered

CURRY POWDER

1 dsp chilli powder
5 dsp coriander powder
2 dsp cumin powder
1 dsp fennel powder
$\frac{1}{2}$ tsp tumeric powder
40 black peppercorns or 1 dsp ground black pepper
10 white peppercorns or 1 tsp ground white pepper
1 tsp cardamon seeds
1 tsp fenugreek seeds

SERVES

4-6

PREPARATION

50 minutes

MALABAR FISH CURRY

The addition of vegetables make this a substantial dish and a serving of plain or tomato rice is all you would need with perhaps a tomato and cucumber relish in yogurt to cool you down.
Essentially a south Indian recipe that has gained enormous popularity amongst the Nonyas with their penchant for spicy and pungent flavours.

METHOD

1. Season fish with 2 tsp salt for 10-15 minutes and set aside. Rinse before cooking.

2. Roughly chop ginger, onions and garlic together in mini food processor.

3. Mix curry powder with a quarter of the coconut milk to make a paste.

4. Heat oil in a saucepan and fry mustard seeds until they pop. Add chopped onion/ginger/garlic and fry to soften. Add curry leaves and cinnamon stick and fry for a minute or two until fragrant.

5. Add curry paste, tamarind juice and water. Bring to the boil.

6. Add quartered vegetables - ladies fingers or aubergines and tomatoes. Simmer for 5 minutes.

7. Add fish and curry leaves and simmer for 8-15 minutes until fish is cooked (length of cooking time will vary with the types and cut of fish used).

8. Add remainder of coconut milk and season with salt to taste.

INGREDIENTS
1¹/₂ lb (700g) firm fish such as salmon or halibut steaks, grey mullet, bream)

10oz (275g) gherkins or pickled cucumbers
1 dsp sugar
¹/₂ tsp salt
4 dsp white vinegar
4oz (110ml) water

REMPAH
1 medium red onion or 10 shallots
3 stalks lemon grass, finely sliced
¹/₂ in galanggal, finely sliced
1 in fresh turmeric or tsp turmeric powder
3 red chillies or 1 dsp chilli powder
1 dsp blachan
8 candlenuts, crushed
3 dsp cooking oil

SERVES
4

PREPARATION
20 minutes

ACHAR IKAN
Spicy braised fish in vinegar and pickled cucumbers.

METHOD
1. Make rempah in a liquidiser.

2. Clean fish, making sure all the scales have been removed. If fish such as grey mullet or mackerel is to be added whole, make a few gashes across to allow the sauce to penetrate.

3. Heat 1 tbsp cooking oil in a deep saucepan and fry rempah until fragrant.

4. Season with salt, sugar and vinegar and top up with water. Bring to the boil and simmer for 5 minutes.

5. Add fish and gherkins and cook for 5-10 minutes, depending on type of fish used until cooked.

6. Adjust seasoning and serve in a deep dish.

INGREDIENTS
2lb (900g) meaty white fish (monkfish, cod, halibut)
1 egg
4oz (110g) coconut powder
1 dsp sugar
1 tsp salt
4 lime leaves finely shredded
12 pieces banana leaves (8in x 4in) or use foil
2 dsp coriander powder
1 tsp turmeric powder

REMPAH
2-6 fresh red chillies (according to taste)*
$\frac{1}{2}$in galanggal, finely sliced
4 stalks lemon grass, finely sliced
2 cloves garlic
10 shallots, finely chopped
1 dsp blachan
3-4fl oz (100ml) water

SERVES
6-8

PREPARATION
30 minutes

OTAK OTAK
Spicy baked fish in banana leaves
Cooking the fish paste in banana leaves does make a big difference to the flavour but the fish paste in itself, flavoured with all the aromatic herbs and spices, is delicious enough. You could therefore cook the paste in ramekin dishes in a bain marie or steamer. This is when the microwave also comes in very handy. Traditionally served with coconut flavoured rice (Nasi lemak), you could serve this as a starter or with main courses.

METHOD
1. Clean fish and remove skin and bone. Pat dry on kitchen paper. Slice thinly.

2. Mince fish in food processor with 1 tsp salt.

3. Make rempah in liquidiser using as little water as is necessary to facilitate blending.

4. Blend rempah, coriander, turmeric and coconut powder with fish in food processor and add lime leaves. Pulse for a few seconds to blend evenly.

5. Cut banana leaves into required sizes and immerse in boiling water for a few seconds to make them more pliable.

6. Spread 1 tbsp of fish paste along the centre of the leaf and seal by tucking the two flaps into the middle. Fasten both ends of the leaf package with cocktail sticks or staples.

7. Grill over a slow charcoal fire for about 15 minutes or under a medium grill for 10 minutes turning over after 5 minutes. Alternatively, bake in hot oven gas mark 7, 425° F (220° C) for 15-20 minutes until fish is cooked.

* If fresh chillies are not available, use 10 dried chillies soaked in hot water for 20 minutes to soften, then drain.

Poultry

HAINAN CHICKEN

AYAM GORENG

OPOR AYAM

AYAM PANGGANG

AYAM SIOH

SOTO AYAM

AYAM TEMPRA

DEVILLED CHICKEN

AYAM BUAHKELUAK

TEOCHEW DUCK

ITEK CHIN

INGREDIENTS

1 ³/₄ lb (800g) chicken
2in ginger, lightly crushed
5 stalks spring onions, tied into a knot
3 cloves of garlic, lightly crushed
1 tbsp sesame oil
6 pints (3.4 litres) water
1 tbsp light soya sauce
2 tsp salt
¹/₂ tsp ground white pepper

GARNISHES

1 cucumber sliced
2 tomatoes, sliced
1 tbsp fried onion rings
1 tbsp chopped coriander leaves

SERVES

4-6

PREPARATION

30 minutes

HAINAN CHICKEN

Steamed chicken flavoured with sesame oil and soya sauce.

This is a classic Singaporean dish and a favourite among all nationalities. It appears to be a plain and blandly cooked chicken, boiled in stock, but eaten with the special flavoured chicken rice and served with chilli and ginger sauce, it is very appetising and memorable. The soup is served together with the rice and drunk in the way Chinese soup is drunk, to refresh the palate and wet the rice. Choose a flavoursome bird to get the best results. Cornfed chickens are best.

METHOD

1. Bring water to the boil in a large stockpot and add whole chicken, crushed ginger, crushed garlic cloves and season with salt and pepper.

2. Simmer chicken on medium heat for 30 minutes until tender.

3. Remove chicken and place on large platter. Rub with sesame oil and light soya sauce. Keep warm.

4. Use some of the chicken stock to cook chicken flavoured rice (see page 54).

5. Reserve remainder of stock and serve as soup, garnished with chopped coriander leaves and fried onion rings. Adjust seasoning with salt and pepper.

6. When rice is cooked and ready to serve, chop chicken into smaller pieces and arrange on platter garnished with freshly sliced cucumber and tomatoes and a few sprigs of coriander leaves. Spoon any juices collected from the sesame and oil marinade over the chopped chicken.

TO SERVE

Reheat remaining stock and season with salt and white pepper and a few dsps of sesame oil. Serve into individual soup bowls garnished with fried onion rings and a sprig of coriander leaf. Use a chilli ginger sauce (see page 134) as a dip for the chicken.

INGREDIENTS
8 chicken thighs (or drumsticks)

MARINADE
2 dsp sesame oil
4 dsp light soya sauce
$1/2$ tsp ground white pepper
I dsp sweet sherry (optional)

Oil for deep frying

GARNISH
Slices of cucumber and tomato

SERVES
4-6

PREPARATION
I5 minutes

A YAM GOREN G
Marinated fried chicken.

Although one of the simplest to cook, this is such a delicious dish and bound to please. I would highly recommend using chicken drumsticks and thigh pieces for succulence after frying as breast meat is not only too dry, but does not absorb the marinade as well. If you prefer, bone the thighs and drumsticks before marinating to allow better absorption and cooking penetration.

METHOD
1. Marinate chicken thighs with sesame oil, light soya sauce, pepper and sherry (if used) for 20 minutes. The marinade should not be left overnight as the meat would be oversalted.

2. Heat oil in deep fryer or wok until smoking and deepfry marinated chicken thighs until cooked through (10-12 minutes). Test by inserting a skewer into the meat - if the juice runs clear and the meat feels tender, it is done.

3. The thighs can be served either whole or chopped into bite-sized pieces and arranged on a platter, garnished with cucumber and tomato slices.

Serve with a dipping sauce made from I tbsp light soya and a drop of sesame oil dip sprinkled with toasted sesame seeds or chilli and garlic sauce (see recipe on page 134).

INGREDIENTS

1 chicken weighing 3½lb (1.5 kg) or 10 chicken thighs
1 stalk lemon grass, trimmed and lightly bruised
8 lime leaves
2oz (50g) coconut powder dissolved in 1 cup hot water
1 dsp sugar
1 tsp turmeric powder
1 pint water

REMPAH

2-3 red chillies, finely sliced
1 medium onion, finely chopped
3 cloves garlic
2 stalk lemon grass, finely sliced
½in galanggal, finely sliced
10 candlenuts, crushed
1 dsp blachan (optional)
1 cup water

SERVES

4-6

PREPARATION

20 minutes

O P O R   A Y A M

Chicken cooked in a spicy lemon grass sauce with coconut

METHOD

1. Cut chicken into smaller pieces. If using chicken thighs, trim excess fat. Put chicken pieces into a deep large saucepan, preferably cast iron.

2. Make rempah in liquidiser.

3. Add rempah mixture to chicken together with remaining ingredients, except coconut milk.

4. Stir to mix evenly and bring to the boil over high heat. Alternatively place in caserole dish and bake in medium oven (Gas mark 6, 400°F (200°C) for 45 minutes, stirring every 20 minutes.

5. If cooking over stove, once the sauce starts to boil, lower heat and simmer for 45 minutes or until chicken is cooked.

6. Stir in coconut cream for the remaining 5 minutes of cooking to prevent curdling. Adjust seasoning and transfer to deep fish for serving.

Opor Ayam is a dish with a profusion of exotic flavours largely dominated by the use of lime leaves and lemon grass and the creaminess of coconut milk. It is deceptively easy to make for a dinner party and can be cooked ahead to leave you free for other tasks.

INGREDIENTS
8 pieces chicken thighs
1 dsp sugar
1 tsp salt (to taste)
4oz (110g) coconut powder mixed to a paste with $^1/_2$ cup hot water
4 tbsp cooking oil

REMPAH
3 stalks lemon grass, finely sliced
$^1/_2$in galanggal, finely sliced
$^1/_2$ tsp ground white pepper
2 red chillies, finely sliced
3 cloves garlic
1in fresh turmeric (or 1 tsp ground turmeric)
10 shallots, finely chopped
juice from 1 large lime

SERVES
4-6

PREPARATION
20 minutes

A YAM PANGGAN G
Balinese barbecued chicken

METHOD
1. Blend rempah in liquidiser with 4 tbsp cooking oil, adding coconut milk if it will help blending.

2. Mix rempah with remainder of ingredients.

3. Make three gashes across the skin of the chicken thighs to help the marinade to seep into the flesh.

4. Rub the marinade into the chicken and leave for at least 2 hours.

5. Barbecue over charcoal brazier or preheat grill to medium high.

6. Cook for 15-20 minutes, turning to prevent burning and baste with leftover marinade.

7. Serve with fresh salad.

INGREDIENTS

1 chicken weighing 3lb (1.35kg) or 10 chicken thighs
4oz (110g) tamarind soaked in 1 cup boiling water to soften and strained to extract 1 cup of thick tamarind juice
1 tbsp malt vinegar
1 medium onion or 10 shallots, finely sliced
2 cloves garlic, finely sliced
1 dsp coriander powder (or use 3 tbsp whole coriander seeds, roasted and ground in coffee mill into a powder)
5 tbsp sugar
2 tbsp dark soya sauce
4 cups water or chicken stock
3 tbsp cooking oil

GARNISH
Fresh coriander leaves
Finely sliced chillies

SERVES
4-6

PREPARATION
30 minutes

A Y A M   S I O H
Chicken cooked in tamarind and coriander

METHOD
1. Marinate chicken pieces overnight in tamarind juice, vinegar, sugar, soya sauce and ground coriander.

2. Chop onions and garlic in mini food processor.

3. Heat oil in heavy saucepan and fry chopped onion and garlic mixture until fragrant.

4. Add marinated chicken pieces and stir to coat evenly.

5. Top up with water and simmer on low to medium heat for 30 minutes.

6. Season with salt and sugar to taste.

7. Remove chicken pieces and brown under a hot grill.

8. Reduce sauce and pour over grilled chicken pieces to serve.

9. Garnish with fresh coriander leaves and finely sliced chillies.

Note: The aroma and flavour of freshly roasted coriander is worth the extra effort .

INGREDIENTS
3lb (1.35kg) chicken
8 pints (4.5 litres) water
1 dsp salt
3 stalks celery

REMPAH
1 medium onion
3 cloves garlic
4 stalks lemon grass
1 tsp ground white pepper
1in fresh turmeric (or 1 tsp ground)
5 candlenuts, crushed
3 tbsp cooking oil

8oz (225g) fresh beansprouts
*rice cakes made with 2 cups grains or use 1lb
(450g) fresh egg noodles*

GARNISHES
1 tbsp fried onion rings
2 stalks spring onions
2 limes, cut into wedges

SERVES
4-6

PREPARATION
45 minutes

S O T O   A Y A M
Indonesian chicken broth flavoured with lemon grass.

METHOD
1. Make rempah in liquidiser and blend to a fine paste.

2. Heat 2 dsp cooking oil in wok or saucepan and fry rempah until fragrant and the oil has separated from the mixture. Set aside.

3. Bring water to the boil and lower the whole chicken into the stock pot. Add fried rempah, leaving as much of the separated oil behind.

4. Add celery and simmer on medium heat for 30 minutes or until the chicken is cooked. Remove chicken from stock and leave to cool.

5. Shred the meat off the bone.

TO ASSEMBLE
1. Blanch beansprouts in a separate saucepan of boiling water and drain.

2. Steam rice cakes or blanch egg noodles (if used).

3. Divide blanched beansprouts and warmed rice cakes or blanched noodles into individual serving bowls, garnished with shredded chicken, fried onion rings, spring onions and a wedge of fresh lime.

4. Put 2-3 ladles of hot chicken soto stock into each bowl and serve with chilli padi sauce (see recipe on page 135).

Soto Ayam is traditionally served with pressed rice cakes or noodles and is a filling and wholesome meal, ideal for luncheon parties and family Sunday lunches. It is mildly spicy but beautifully aromatic. A side dish of fiery bird's eye chillies is usually served to those who like more pungency in their soup.

INGREDIENTS

1lb (450g) breast of chicken, thinly sliced into
1$\frac{1}{2}$in strips
6-8 fresh lime leaves
2-3 cloves garlic, thinly sliced or chopped
1 dsp fish sauce
1 dsp dark soya
1 dsp sugar
2 dsp vegetable cooking oil
salt and pepper to taste
$\frac{1}{2}$ cup water or chicken stock
1 fresh red chilli, sliced diagonally

SERVES

2-4 as part of main course

PREPARATION

15 minutes

A Y A M   T E M P R A

The Nonya version of a dish by this name does not in fact include kaffir lime leaves as the main ingredient but I happened to put this dish together and it works really well. Instead of using lime juice, I swapped it for lime leaves which I felt is less sharp and more fragrant.

Although this is an incredibly easy and straightforward dish to make, the flavours are so aromatic that it belies its simplicity.

Photograph (top right) opposite.

METHOD

1. Heat cooking oil in wok or saucepan and lightly brown sliced or chopped garlic.

2. Add sliced chicken pieces and stir to seal the meat and to prevent sticking.

3. Add sauces and season with sugar, salt and pepper.

4. Add lightly torn lime leaves and sliced chillies and stir to mix.

5. The juices from the chicken should be sufficient to produce a thin sauce but if the heat is intense and the chicken is sticking to the wok, add chicken stock one spoonful at a time.

6. Cook for 5-6 minutes until chicken is cooked. Serve immediately on a warm serving dish. However, it can be left in the pan until required and reheated.

Devilled Chicken, above left, is made with a complex rempah and has strong flavours. In contrast, Ayam Tempra, right, is a light stirfry dish but nevertheless equally delicious.

INGREDIENTS

8 chicken thighs
1 large onion, thinly sliced
3 cloves garlic, thinly sliced
3 slices fresh ginger
2 tomatoes, quartered
1 dsp English mustard
2 dsp vinegar
1 dsp brown sugar
1 tsp salt, to taste
2 dsp cooking oil

REMPAH
6 shallots
6 dried chillies
1 clove garlic
4 candlenuts, crushed
1 tsp blachan
1 tsp turmeric powder
3 dsp cooking oil

GARNISH
Fresh parsley

SERVES
4-6

PREPARATION
30 minutes

DEVILLED CHICKEN

This is a Eurasian dish with Portuguese influence. I have eaten several versions of so-called devilled chicken but this is the recipe that I like best. It is rather pungent but feel free to tone it down to suit your taste. It can also be made with pork steaks.
Photograph (left) page 95.

METHOD

1. Blend rempah in a mini food processor until fine. If using a liquidiser, add scant water to facilitate grinding.

2. Rub chicken pieces with salt and shallow fry in 4 tbsp cooking oil to crispen the skin. Set aside.

3. Heat 2 dsp cooking oil in a saucepan and lightly brown sliced onions and ginger slices.

4. Add rempah and stir to prevent sticking and burning. Add chicken pieces and stir to coat the chicken with the spices.

5. Add sugar, mustard, salt and vinegar and 1 cup water. Lower heat and simmer covered, for 20 minutes until chicken is tender, stirring occasionally to prevent sticking at the bottom and burning. Adjust seasoning at the end of the cooking time. Serve hot garnished with parsley.

INGREDIENTS

1 chicken weighing about 4 lbs (1.8kg) cut into smaller pieces

8oz (225g) minced pork
20 buah keluak (soaked for 24 hours)
2 tbsp tamarind soaked with 1 cup boiling water and strained to extract juices
2 dsp sugar
1 tsp salt
3 dsp dark soya sauce
3 tbsp cooking oil

REMPAH

$1^1/_2$in fresh turmeric or $1^1/_2$ tsp turmeric powder
3 cloves garlic
1 medium onion, finely chopped
3 stalks lemon grass, thinly sliced
$^1/_2$in galanggal, finely sliced
8 fresh red chillies (1 dsp chilli powder)
8 candlenuts
1 dsp blachan

SERVES

4-6

PREPARATION

45 minutes

A Y A M
B U A H   K E L U A K

Although it is unlikely that this dish will find its way to the European table, a Nonya recipe book will be incomplete without it. Flavoured with an Indonesian nut called buah keluak, it has a distinctive earthy flavour and is an acquired taste. However, as with so many foods that take getting used to, once acquired, always drooled over.

METHOD

1. Make rempah in liquidiser by blending with 3 tbsp cooking oil and scant water to facilitate grinding.

2. Make a small opening by chipping away at the top end of the nut with a hammer, taking care to leave the shell intact for stuffing.

3. Remove the soft flesh from the nut. Save 2 tbsp buah keluak. Mix remainder with 2 dsp of rempah mixture, pork mince and season with 1 tsp salt and 1 tsp sugar in a food processor.

4. Put stuffing back into shell.

5. Heat 2 tbsp cooking oil in deep large saucepan, cast iron preferably, and fry remaining rempah until fragrant. Add the 2 dsp buah keluak that has not been added to the stuffing.

6. Add chicken pieces and stir to coat evenly.

7. Add tamarind juice and water, stirring to mix.

8. Season with soy sauce, salt and pepper. Throw in stuffed nuts and simmer over medium heat for 30 to 45 minutes until chicken is tender.

9. Serve in large casserole dish. The delicious sauce is spooned over to flavour plain steamed rice and the stuffing in the nut is scooped out using the back of a fork or table knife, the sauce and the nut being savoured more than the chicken meat.

INGREDIENTS

3lbs (1.35kg) duck or a pair of magret
$^1/_2$ tsp fivespice powder
2 tbsp dark soya sauce
2-3 star anise
1 tbsp vinegar
4-5 cups stock or water
4-5 slices galanggal
3 cloves garlic, leave skin on and lightly crush
1 tsp salt
2 tbsp sugar

GARNISH
Fresh coriander leaves or
Spring onion curls

SERVES
4-6

PREPARATION
20 minutes

TEOCHEW DUCK
Soya braised duck with star anise

METHOD

1. Rub fivespice powder into the skin of the duck or magret, both inside and out. Marinate for an hour or so.

2. Fry sugar in wok or saucepan until it starts to caramelise. Add garlic and galanggal and stir.

3. Add 1 cup of water and dark soya sauce. The sugar will solidify on contact with the cold water and form hard lumps but this should dissolve with further cooking.

4. Lower duck into the pan and coat duck with the sauce.

5. Add remaining water or stock and star anise.

6. Bring to the boil and simmer for 45 minutes or so until duck is tender.

7. To serve, drain duck and chop into bite-sized pieces. Arrange onto platter and spoon sauce over or serve sauce separately in sauceboat.

Garnish with fresh coriander leaves or finely sliced spring onions cut length-wise so that they form curls.

Crispy Peking duck so dominates the Chinese banqueting scene that some of the more delectable duck recipes get forgotten. Save yourself the arduous task of blow-drying duck in order to crispen the skin. Instead, serve this recipe of braised duck which is a delicacy of the Quangdong province of China. The addition of galanggal slices is undoubtedly a Nonya influence.

INGREDIENTS

3lb (1.35kg) duck cut into smaller pieces

2 tbsp tauceo mashed into a paste with a fork

4 cloves garlic, finely sliced and chopped in a food processor with 12 shallots or 1 medium red onion

1 in ginger lightly crushed
6 tbsp cooking oil
3 tbsp coriander seeds, roasted and ground to a powder
2 tbsp dark soya sauce
8oz (220ml) water
1 tsp ground white pepper
2 tbsp sugar
1 tsp salt to taste

GARNISH

Fresh coriander leaves

SERVES

4-6

PREPARATION

30 minutes

ITEK CHIN

Braised duck in soya beans and spiced with coriander. A fine example of the Chinese and Malay marriage of ingredients that works remarkably well. Can also be made with pork.

METHOD

1. Heat oil in large heavy saucepan and fry onion and garlic mixture until fragrant.

2. Add tauceo, ginger and coriander and fry for another minute.

3. Add duck pieces and fry to coat evenly, scraping the bottom well to prevent sticking and burning.

4. Add sugar and pepper and top up with water, stirring into the bottom to mix evenly.

5. Add salt to taste and replace lid to cover. Simmer on medium heat for 45 minutes

6. Check for water level every 15 minutes or so, adding $\frac{1}{2}$ cup at a time. The gravy should be slightly thick and not too watery.

7. Serve when duck is tender, garnished with fresh coriander leaves.

PORK BEEF AND LAMB

TULANG BABI CHUEY TAUSEE

DAGING KECHAP

BABI PONGTAY

BABI TAUYU

BABI ASSAM MANIS

KALIO

RENDANG

DAGING CHILLI PADI

KURMAH

CURRY KAMBING

DAGING TAUCEO

INGREDIENTS
2 lb (900g) spare ribs, chopped into bitesized pieces

MARINADE
1 tbsp salted black beans, rinsed and chopped
$\frac{1}{2}$in fresh ginger, finely chopped
3 cloves garlic, chopped
2 red chillies, thinly sliced
1 dsp dark soya sauce
1 dsp sugar
1 dsp sesame oil
1 dsp sherry
1 dsp oyster sauce (optional)
1 dsp cornflour

GARNISH
2 stalks spring onions, chopped

SERVES
4-6

PREPARATION
15 minutes

INGREDIENTS
8oz (225g) rump steak, sliced paper thin
4 cloves garlic, crushed
2 dsp sugar
pinch of salt, to taste
1 tbsp dark soya sauce
pinch of ground white paper
2 dsp cooking oil

SERVES
2-4

PREPARATION
10 minutes

TULANG BABI CHUEY TAUSEE
Steamed pork spare ribs in chilli beans.
Photograph on page 105.

METHOD
1. Marinate spare ribs with marinade ingredients for 12 hours.

2. Place on shallow bowl and steam for 25-30 minutes until cooked.

3. Garnish with chopped spring onions.

TO MAKE YOUR OWN STEAMER
You will need a large deep saucepan or wok. Fill with 2 pints of water and place a perforated metal plate (steamer) or raise the bowl above the water level with a pudding basin or metal basin turned upside down. Cover and bring to the boil.

DAGING KECHAP
Beef slices stirfried with garlic and dark soya.

I have served this to some of my friends and staff and it has never failed to please. In fact they are quite astonished when I tell them how quick and easy it is to make.

METHOD
1. Heat oil in wok or saucepan and lightly brown garlic, stirring to prevent it from sticking and burning.

2. Add beef slices and stir to mix evenly and to seal the meat.

3. Add seasonings and stir, cook for a further 2 minutes and serve.

INGREDIENTS

2 1/2 lb (1 kg) pork steaks (do not trim fat) cut into 2 x 1 in cubes
5 tbsp dark soya sauce
1/2 tsp ground white pepper
1 tsp salt
2 dsp sugar
2 dsp tauceo, mashed with a fork
8-10 dried Chinese mushrooms, soaked in 1 cup boiling water to soften
6 potatoes peeled and quartered
4oz (110g) bamboo shoot slices
2 pints (1 litre) water or chicken stock
2in stick cinnamon
5 cloves

REMPAH
1 medium onion finely chopped
3 cloves of garlic
Blend in liquidiser with 1 tbsp of cooking oil

GARNISH
Fresh coriander leaves

SERVES

6-8

PREPARATION

20 minutes

BABI PONGTAY

A typically Nonya dish which combines Chinese-style braised pork with the aromatics of onions, ginger and garlic, spiced with cloves and cinnamon. Traditionally made with pig's trotters, this has been adapted for pork steaks. It can also be made with chicken pieces.

METHOD

1. Heat 2 tbsp oil in large deep saucepan, preferably cast iron, and fry rempah until fragrant. Add cloves and cinnamon.

2. Add tauceo and pork pieces and fry to coat evenly and prevent sticking.

3. Add bamboo shoot slices and Chinese mushrooms and season with soya sauce, sugar, white pepper and salt to taste.

4. Top up with chicken stock or water and simmer on medium heat for 30 minutes until pork is almost tender.

5. Add potatoes and cook for a further 20 minutes. Adding potatoes also helps to thicken the sauce whilst padding out the dish.

6. Serve in tureen or deep dish, garnish with fresh coriander leaves.

INGREDIENTS

2lbs (900g) leg of pork, cut into cubes
6 hardboiled eggs, shelled
6 large potatoes, peeled and quartered
10 cloves garlic, lightly crushed
$^1/_2$ tsp fivespice powder
1 cup dark soya sauce
2 tbsp sugar
2 tsp salt (to taste)
$^1/_2$ tsp ground white pepper
2 pints (1.2 litres) water
2oz (50g) Chinese dried mushrooms,
soaked to soften (optional)

SERVES

6-8

PREPARATION

20 minutes

BABI TAUYU

Braised pork in garlic and soya sauce.

METHOD

1. Hardboil eggs for 12 minutes and place under cold running water. Remove shell and set aside.

2. Put pork pieces into a large saucepan and add thick dark soya sauce, fivespice powder, sugar and crushed garlic. If you like pork skin, do not trim the pieces as the fat underneath the skin adds extra flavour and the chewy skin is actually quite delicious.

3. Mix well and cook in a covered saucepan on minimum heat for 20 minutes stirring every so often to prevent sticking. The juices from the pork will soon start to run and there should be enough moisture in the saucepan by then to allow you to leave it to cook in its own steam. If this is not the case (the heat being too high and the moisture evaporated away), add $^1/_2$ cup of water to help things along. The reason for not adding too much water at this early stage is to allow the soya sauce to seep into the meat.

4. As soon as the meat looks dark enough, top it up with the remainder of the liquid and bring to a simmering boil. Continue to cook over medium low heat for 20 minutes.

5. Add potato chunks and dried mushrooms if used (or use small new potatoes) and cook for a further 20 minutes.

4. During the last 5 minutes of cooking, add hardboiled eggs and simmer until meat is tender.

Babi Tauyu is a classic Hokkien dish not dissimilar to the Cantonese redcooked pork. The flavour of garlic and soya sauce is completely absorbed by slow cooking and every mouthful is exquisitely flavoursome. There are also several variations to this dish by the addition of Chinese mushrooms, potatoes, hard boiled eggs, red dates and chestnuts. The Nonyas usually serve sambal blachan as a side dish to add pungency to an otherwise non-spicy Chinese classic.

INGREDIENTS

1lb (450g) pork tenderloin, cut across the length into ¼in slices
Cheaper pork leg steaks can be used but these tend to be less tender

MARINADE
2 dsp light soya sauce
sprinkling of salt and ground white pepper

2-3 dsp cornflour (to coat)

SAUCE
3 dsp tomato ketchup
1 dsp light brown or demerara sugar
1 small onion cut into rings
2 cloves garlic, thinly sliced
1in ginger cut into julienne strips
1 dsp medium sherry
1 dsp malt or wine vinegar
4oz (110g) tin unsweetened pineapple pieces and juice
sprinkling of salt and ground white pepper to taste

½ tsp crushed dried chillies or ½ tsp chilli powder (optional)
2 dsp cooking oil

2 cups oil for shallow frying

SERVES
2-4 as part of main course

PREPARATION
20 minutes

BABI ASSAM MANIS
The Nonya influence is clearly evident in this delicious classic dish of sweet and sour pork spiked with chillies and enriched with tropical fruit.

METHOD
1. Cut pork tenderloin across the length into 1/4 inch rings.

2. Add marinade ingredients and leave for 20 minutes.

3. Dust liberally with cornfour and shallow or deep fry until crisp.

4. Transfer onto kitchen paper to drain excess oil. Keep warm in low oven.

TO MAKE THE SAUCE
1. Heat 2 dsp vegetable cooking oil in saucepan.

2. Add julienned ginger, sliced garlic and onion rings and stirfry for 5-6 minutes until the onions are beginning to brown at the edges.

3. Add remainder of sauce ingredients. Leave out chillies altogether if you prefer to have a sauce that is not pungent or adjust the amount of chillies according to taste.

4. Simmer over medium heat for a minute or two until sauce has thickened and pour over crispy pork when ready to serve. If the sauce is poured over the pork too far in advance, the crispy texture of the pork slices is lost and the dish would be soggy.

INGREDIENTS
1lb (450g) braising steak, cut into bitesized chunks
8oz (225g) coconut powder dissolved in 1 cup hot water
2 tbsp cooking oil
1 tsp salt
$1^3/_4$ pints (1 litre) water

REMPAH
2 stalks lemon grass, finely sliced
10 shallots, chopped
6 cloves garlic, chopped
2in ginger, finely sliced
2in galanggal, finely sliced,
6 large red chillies, finely sliced
10 candlenuts, crushed
4 tbsp cooking oil

POWDERED INGREDIENTS
1 tbsp coriander powder
1 tsp ground black pepper
4 tbsp chopped palm sugar

SERVES
4

PREPARATION
30 minutes

KALIO
Indonesian braised beef

My father was of Indonesian-Chinese origin, another hybrid of Chinese settlers and Indonesian wives. Undoubtedly, my mother's culinary repertoire encompassed recipes from his culinary background. This is one of his favourite dishes.

METHOD
1. Make rempah by blending rempah ingredients to a fine paste in liquidiser using 4 tbsp cooking oil to lubricate the blades. Remove from blender and mix in powdered ingredients.

2. Heat cooking oil in a heavy based saucepan and fry rempah mixture until fragrant and the oil has separated from the mixture.

3. Add beef chunks and stir to coat the pieces evenly with the spice mixture.

4. Top up with water and simmer on low heat for 45 minutes until beef is tender. Alternatively, reduce the amount of water and bake in a preheated oven for 45-60 minutes, gas mark 6, 200°C (400°F).

5. During the last 10 minutes of cooking, add salt and coconut milk. Skim off excess oil before serving.

INGREDIENTS

2lbs (900g) beef (chuck or braising
steak), cut into 1in cubes
8 dsp cooking oil
10 lime leaves
2 lemon grass, lightly bruised
1 dsp sugar
1 tsp salt (to taste)
4oz (10ml) desiccated coconut, browned
2 pints beef stock (or water)

REMPAH
4 stalks lemon grass, thinly sliced
4 cloves of garlic
2 medium onions
8 candlenuts
$1/2$ in ginger
1 in galanggal, thinly sliced
$1/2$ cup water

2 tbsp coriander powder
1 tsp cumin powder
$1/2$ tsp fennel powder
$1/4$ tsp turmeric
2 dsp chilli powder

SERVES
4-6

PREPARATION
45 minutes

RENDANG

The classic Indonesian beef curry, rendang is very popular in Malaysia and
Singapore and countless hybrid recipes exist. It improves with age and hence is
ideally cooked the day before intended consumption.
Photograph (left) page 109.

METHOD

1. Heat cooking oil and brown meat in small batches. Set aside.

2. Blend rempah ingredients in liquidiser. When a fine paste is achieved, transfer into a large mixing bowl and add powdered spices, mixing thoroughly.

3. Fry this mixture until fragrant in the same saucepan that has been used to brown the meat.

4. Add the browned meat and mix with the rempah until the meat is thoroughly coated.

5. Add boiling stock, lime leaves and lemon grass stalks.

6. Simmer over medium heat for $1\frac{1}{2}$ hours.

7. Meanwhile, blend the browned desiccated coconut in a little water and liquidise to a fine paste.

8. Add this mixture to the rendang and continue cooking.

9. When the meat is tender (approximately 1 hour), add sugar and salt to taste.

10. Skim off excess oil before serving.

DAGING CHILLI PADI

Beef steaks marinated in hot bird's eye chillies.

Be forewarned this is a seriously hot dish but if you are immune to chillies as I am, it is incredibly delicious and more'ish. I used to show off my prowess as a six year old by chewing on a bird's eye chilli. After that nothing is ever hot enough for me. Of course, there is nothing to stop you from toning down the dish. As the beef is actually boiled until it is tenderised, you can use an inexpensive cut of braising beef or topside.

METHOD

1. Boil the braising steak as a whole and simmer for an hour until it is fully tenderised. Leave to cool and then cut into $1/_2$in steaks.

2. Remove the tails of the bird's eye chillies and pop them into a mini food processor or liquidiser with the oil, fresh garlic, sugar and salt and soya sauce. Liquidise to a fine paste.

3. Marinate the steaks in the chilli paste for at least 30 minutes and cook on a preheated hot grill or barbecue over charcoal for 5 minutes on either side. Serve garnished with fresh salad leaves.

INGREDIENTS

$1^1/_2$ lb (700g) braising beef
2 tbsp bird's eye chillies
6 cloves fresh garlic
1 tbsp dark soya sauce
2 tbsp palm sugar (substitute with dark brown sugar)
$1/_2$ tsp salt
1 tbsp cooking oil
2 pints (1.2 litres) water

GARNISH
Fresh salad leaves

SERVES
4-6

PREPARATION
20 minutes

INGREDIENTS

3 lb (1.35kg) lamb, cut into cubes
1 large onion, finely sliced
3 cloves garlic, finely sliced
$\frac{1}{2}$in ginger, finely sliced
1 tbsp curry leaves
2oz (50g) butter or ghee
2 dsp cooking oil
$1\frac{3}{4}$ pint (1 litre) water
10 cardamon pods
2 star anise
2in stick cinnamon
8 cloves
6 potatoes
4oz (110g) ground almonds
6-10 green chillies (to taste)
10oz (275ml) yogurt
4oz (110g) coconut powder mixed with 1 cup
hot water
$1\frac{1}{2}$-2 tsp salt to taste

POWDERED INGREDIENTS

1 tbsp coriander
1 tsp cumin
$\frac{1}{2}$ tsp fennel
1 tsp ground black pepper
1 tsp turmeric
$\frac{1}{2}$ nutmeg (finely grated)

GARNISH
Fresh coriander leaves

SERVES
4-6

PREPARATION
15 minutes

K U R M A H

Undoubtedly an adaptation of the Indian version, lamb is cooked in a myriad of spices, enriched with coconut milk. You could substitute lamb for chicken - just reduce the cooking time to 20-25 minutes.

METHOD

1. Cut lamb into 1in cubes and marinate with powdered ingredients for at least an hour.

2. Heat ghee or butter mixed with cooking oil in a large heavy saucepan such as Le Creuset.

3. Add finely chopped onions and garlic (and curry leaves if used) and sauté for 2-3 minutes until softened.

4. Add cardamons, cloves, cinnamon stick and star anise.

5. Add marinated lamb and sliced green chillies and stir to coat evenly.

6. Add water and stir, making sure the bottom is not sticking.

7. Reduce heat to medium low, cover and allow the kurmah to simmer for 45 minutes.

8. Add potatoes and give the kurmah another stir, checking the consistency. If you think it is drying too quickly, add a cup or two of water to prevent sticking. Continue cooking for 15-20 minutes until potatoes and lamb are tender.

9. Add almonds, yogurt and coconut milk during the last stage of cooking to thicken the sauce and cook under a low heat for another 15-20 minutes.

10. Season with salt to taste.

11. Transfer to serving dish and sprinkle with fresh coriander leaves to garnish.

INGREDIENTS

3 lbs(1.35kg) lamb steaks, cut into 1in cubes
4 tomatoes, quartered
4 tbsp cooking oil
1 tsp salt, to taste
8oz (225g) coconut powder, dissolved in 1 cup water
2 tbsp curry powder

REMPAH
1 large red onion
3 cloves garlic
1in ginger

SERVES
4-6

PREPARATION
30 minutes

CURRY KAMBING
Dry lamb curry.

METHOD

1. Marinate the lamb pieces in the curry powder for at least 30 minutes.

2. Roughly chop onions, garlic and ginger in a food processor for 10-15 seconds without reducing it into a pulp.

3. Heat cooking oil in a heavy based saucepan and brown the onion mixture.

4. Add the marinated lamb pieces and quartered tomatoes and stir to prevent sticking.

5. Top up with 1 cup coconut milk and simmer on low heat for 45 minutes until lamb is tender. You will need to stir frequently, scraping the bottom to prevent sticking and burning and gradually add a tablespoon of water at a time if it gets too dry.

INGREDIENTS

1lb (450g) rump or fillet steak, thinly sliced
2 cloves garlic, thinly sliced or chopped
6 shallots, thinly sliced
6 slices galanggal, thinly sliced
1 red chilli, thinly sliced diagonally
1 dsp yellow bean paste
1 dsp sugar
1 dsp dark soya
1 dsp fish sauce (optional)
2 tbsp vegetable cooking oil
$^1/_2$ cup of stock

SERVES

2-4

PREPARATION

15 minutes

DAGING TAUCEO

Beef slices stirfried with galanggal and chillies.
The unique fragrance of galanggal is clearly evident in this easy stirfry beef dish.

METHOD

1. Heat cooking oil in wok or saucepan and lightly brown shallots, garlic and galanggal.

2. Add beef slices and stirfry to seal meat as well as prevent sticking.

3. Sprinkle with stock if the heat is too intense and the meat is sticking to the pot.

4. Add sauces and seasonings to taste.

5. Add sliced chillies and cook for a minute or two until beef is cooked.

6. Transfer to warm serving dish or leave in saucepan until required.

CakeS and DessertS

PENGAT PISANG

KUEH DADAR

PULOT HITAM

PULOT INTI

KUEH BENGKANG

ONDEH ONDEH

KUEH LAPIS

SAGO MELAKA

AGAR AGAR

COCONUT SAGO

BUBUR CHA CHA

PULOT SERIKAYA

LYCHEE ICE CREAM

MANGO ICE CREAM

INGREDIENTS

8-10 ripe bananas
16oz (450g) tinned jackfruit (optional)
2oz (50g) pearl sago, soaked in 1 cup
water
1 pint water
16oz (450g) tinned coconut milk
6oz (175g) palm sugar boiled with 1 cup
water for syrup
pinch of salt
4 pandan leaves (if available)

SERVES

4-6

PREPARATION

15 minutes

PENGAT PISANG

Stewed bananas in coconut milk flavoured with palm sugar.

This is a delicious banana dessert which is cooked in a combination of coconut milk and palm sugar. Great for a dinner party as it can be made in advance and either served cold or hot, warmed up just before serving.

In southeast Asia where tropical fruits are in abundance, jackfruits and chempedak are added for extra flavour. If you have ever had these fruits, you will drool in their memory. They lose their flavour in canning and are poor substitutes but the texture is probably worth savouring.

METHOD

1. Make gula melaka (palm sugar) syrup by boiling in water until dissolved and strain to remove foreign bodies.

2. Rinse and drain soaked pearl sago.

3. Peel and halve bananas.

4. Wash pandan leaves and run a fork through to release the essence and tie into a knot.

5. Bring water and pandan leaves to the boil and add sago until it turns transparent.

6. Add bananas, jackfruit (if used), coconut milk and palm sugar and simmer on low heat for 5 minutes until bananas are softened.

7. Serve cold or hot.

Desserts are seldom served after a rich Nonya meal. Instead, fresh tropical fruits that cleanse the palate and sweeten the breath are preferred. Spoilt for choice, southeast Asia has many fruits that are unheard of in Europe. Temperate and citrus fruits are also easily available to add to the endless variety and Chinese lychees and longans flood the markets when in season.
If you insist on serving something exotic, the desserts given on the following pages are appropriate but in Southeast Asia they are more likely to be eaten as snacks or tea-time treats.

INGREDIENTS

FILLING
1 grated coconut, dark skin removed
3 tbsp sugar
8oz (225g) palm sugar (gula melaka), chopped
1 cup water
3 pandan leaves

BATTER
4oz (110g) plain flour, sifted
2 cups coconut milk, extracted from $^1/_2$ grated coconut and $1^1/_2$ cups of water
1 egg, beaten
pinch of salt
$^1/_2$ tsp rose colouring or 2 tbsp extract of pandan leaves

SERVES
4-6

PREPARATION
30 minutes

K U E H   D A D A R
Coconut pancake.
Photograph on page 115.

METHOD
FILLING
1. Dissolve chopped palm sugar in water in saucepan over low heat. Strain through wire sieve.

2. Return dissolved and strained palm sugar to the saucepan and reduce consistency to half. Add grated coconut and sugar and mix well. Run a fork through pandan leaves, tie into a knot and add to the coconut mixture. Cook slowly until coconut is fairly dry. Cool.

This coconut candy or inti (Malay) can be used for various Malay confections and cakes and is the filling for Kueh dadar (Coconut pancakes).

BATTER
If green colouring is desired, liquidise 6-8 chopped pandan leaves with $^1/_2$ a cup of water and squeeze through a sieve with fingers for the juice, which not only provides the green colouring but also flavours the batter with its vanilla-like fragrance. You will need at least 2 tbsp of juice.

1. Mix flour, egg, salt and coconut milk until smooth, either in a liquidiser or manually. Add colouring.

2. Heat frying pan and brush lightly with cooking oil or butter. Pour in 2 tbsp batter at a time and make thin layers of pancakes. Do not brown the pancakes.

TO ASSEMBLE
3. Transfer onto flat surface.

4. Put 1 tbsp of filling in the middle, tuck the sides in and roll.

Can be served warm or cold.

INGREDIENTS

2 cups black glutinous rice, soaked overnight
3-4 pandan leaves to flavour
6 cups water
$\frac{1}{2}$ cup granulated white sugar, to taste
8oz (225g) coconut powder dissolved in 1 cup hot water (or use 16oz [450g] tinned coconut milk)

SERVES

4-6

PREPARATION

10 minutes

PULOT HITAM

Serving black glutinous rice pudding with thick coconut cream is analogous to the European Ambrosia rice pudding. The fragrance and aroma of black glutinous rice is however much more ambrosial and the addition of fresh coconut cream is like heavenly nectar.

Use fresh coconut cream if you have the time and inclination to prepare your own - otherwise make do with the powdered instant or tinned version.
Photograph on page 115.

METHOD

1. Wash rice through several changes of water in the cooking saucepan and discard any chaff or foreign material that floats to the top.

2. Top up with water and bring to the boil.

3. Wash pandan leaves and run a fork down their length to release the fragrance. Tie into a knot and add to the boiling rice.

4. Simmer over low heat for 45 minutes until tender, stirring every now and then to prevent sticking.

5. Sweeten with sugar just before serving.

6. Serve hot, topped with thick coconut cream.

Note: Soaking the rice overnight would reduce cooking time. Alternatively cook in a pressure cooker for 30 minutes or micro-wave on high for 20 minutes.

INGREDIENTS

2 cups glutinous rice
16oz (450ml) tinned coconut milk
4oz (110ml) water
pinch of salt

FILLING
$^1/_2$ fresh coconut
4 tbsp brown sugar
4oz (110g) gula melaka (palm sugar)
4 tbsp water
3 pandan leaves

SERVES
4-6

PREPARATION
30 minutes

PULOT INTI
Steamed glutinous rice with a coconut topping.

You might find this too heavy as a dessert but it is a delicious mid-morning snack or served with tea.
Inti is the Malay term for the palm sugar flavoured desiccated coconut. It is used in a number of Nonya kuehs and cakes. Make a large batch as it keeps for weeks in the refrigerator or can be frozen so that it is available for other desserts and cakes. It is also used as a filling for coconut pancakes called Kueh dadar. The glutinous rice should be soaked overnight to tenderise. Use banana leaves (if available) to wrap into little parcels for authentic presentation.
Photograph opposite.

METHOD

1. Rinse glutinous rice (pulot) in water several times and soak overnight. Rinse again thoroughly before use and drain well.

2. Place pulot in steaming container and add coconut milk, salt and water.

3. Prepare steamer (either using a wok or placed over a trivet in pressure cooker or saucepan) and steam pulut for 25-30 minutes until cooked. Alternatively, cook in microwave for 15 minutes on high.

4. While the pulot is cooking, prepare the filling by boiling the sugar, palm sugar and water for 15 minutes until all the sugar has dissolved.

5. Add fresh grated coconut and cook until the mixture thickens.

6. Remove pulot from steamer and allow to cool. Cut into small serving pieces and top with the inti.

INGREDIENTS

4 cups grated tapioca
2 tbsp plain flour
I cup sugar
I white grated coconut
2 eggs, beaten
2oz (50g) butter
4 tbsp evaporated milk
pinch of salt

SERVES

6-8

PREPARATION

25 minutes

KUEH BENGKANG

Baked tapioca cake.

If you have ever wondered what to do with the fresh tapioca that has been spotted on the shelves of the large supermarket chain, try this recipe for a teatime snack. You would however need to try your hand at grating your own coconut for best results. Alternatively, use dried desiccated coconut and add tinned coconut milk to supplement the flavour.
Photograph (top) page 119.

METHOD

1. Peel the brown skin off the tapioca and either grate manually on a metal grater, or cut into small pieces and chop in a food processor until fine.

2. Mix grated tapioca with grated coconut, butter, sugar, evaporated and coconut milk and egg, leaving a little for glazing.

3. Grease a 9in x 7in square baking tin and spread tapioca mixture evenly into it. Brush with a glazing of beaten egg.

4. Bake in a hot preheated oven (Gas mark 6,200°C/400°F) for 40 minutes until dry and browned.

5. Remove from oven and leave to cool. Cut into $^1/_2$in serving slices and serve cold.

INGREDIENTS
1lb (450g) glutinous rice flour
6 pandan leaves, chopped
10oz (275g) palm sugar (gula melaka), chopped
1 fresh coconut, grated
pinch of salt

2 pints (1 litre) boiling water

SERVES
4-6

PREPARATION
45 minutes

ONDEH ONDEH
Glutinous rice balls rolled in freshly grated coconut.

Here is another recipe that is quite fun to make despite being somewhat laborious. This is probably one reason why my mother used to get the children involved so as to lighten the load and get us out of mischief. When my brothers and sisters were growing up in the sixties, television had not arrived in Singapore and we were usually at a loss during the hazy afternoons when it was too hot to play out (school was only in the mornings).
I love the delicious feeling of oozing gula melaka syrup as you bite through the dough. The traditional Nonya recipe uses mashed sweet potatoes but I have found that this is not only tedious but the variety of sweet potatoes available in the West is not suitable. Glutinous rice powder is an excellent substitute and works well for me.
Photograph on page 119.

METHOD
1. Chop 6 pandan leaves and blend in a liquidiser with $1/_2$ cup of water until fine. Strain through a sieve and squeeze to extract juice.

2. Add pandan extract gradually to the glutinous rice flour until well blended and a manageable dough is obtained.

3. Take one dessertspoonful of dough and roll into a ball. Flatten and insert a small lump of chopped gula melaka into it. Seal to enclose the gula melaka and roll into a ball. Repeat until dough is used up.

4. Boil water in a deep saucepan and drop sweet potato balls into it a few at a time. Remove with a slotted spoon when they rise to the surface and roll them immediately onto freshly grated coconut sprinkled with a pinch of salt.

Best served freshly made. Refrigeration is recommended if not served immediately as the fresh grated coconut tends to turn rancid quite quickly. However, the dough then becomes stiff. Reheat in microwave for 10 seconds after refrigeration to soften the dough.

INGREDIENTS
5oz (150 g) rice flour
10oz (300 g) tapioca starch flour
12oz (350 g) sugar
32oz (900ml) tinned coconut milk
2 tsp salt
10 pandan leaves
colouring

SERVES
8 or more

PREPARATION
30 minutes

K U E Y   L A P I S
Rainbow layer cake.
You would need a double boiler for efficient steaming. It is fairly simple to make but the layering can be time-consuming.
Photograph (bottom right) page 126.

METHOD
1. Make a syrup by boiling sugar in 2 cups of water for 5 minutes. Run a fork through 3 pandan leaves, tie them into a knot and boil with the sugar syrup to flavour. Leave to cool.

2. Liquidise the remaining pandan leaves in a mini food processor with $1/2$ cup of water for 2 minutes. Strain over a sieve and squeeze to extract juice. Set aside.

3. Mix rice flour and tapioca starch into a bowl with the cooled syrup. Add coconut cream and salt and stir to blend evenly.

4. Divide into 3 separate containers (assuming 3 colours are desired).

5. Add 2-3 drops of food colouring in each container, using the pandan extract to colour and flavour one lot.

6. Bring a double boiler to the boil and lower a greased 7in souffle dish into it.

7. Pour 2 tablespoonfuls of batter into the dish and steam for 3 minutes until it has set.

8. Add 2 tablespoonfuls of the next coloured batter and steam for a further 3 minutes until set. Repeat the procedure with different coloured layers until all the batter has been used up.

9. Steam the last layer for a further 15 minutes. Leave to cool.

10. When cooled, loosen the edges with a palette knife and transfer onto serving dish.

INGREDIENTS
10oz (275g) sago pearls
12 cups water
6 pandan leaves
14 fl oz (375ml) tinned coconut milk
8oz (225g) palm sugar, boiled with 1 cup water
to make syrup

Serves
4

Preparation
15 minutes

S A G O   M E L A K A

This is a favourite dessert amongst Nonyas who are particularly fond of anything made with coconut. Combined with the rich palm sugar, the delicious sauce adds a new dimension to the otherwise bland tasting sago pearls.
You should use freshly made coconut milk for best flavour but the tinned version is used here for convenience.

METHOD
1. Wash pandan leaves and run a fork through to release the essence. Use 3 leaves for flavouring syrup and the other 3 to flavour the sago.

2. Soak sago in a bowl of water for 20 minutes and rinse through sieve to remove excess starch. Drain.

3. Boil water in a large saucepan and add sago and pandan leaves. Simmer for 10 minutes, stirring the bottom to prevent sticking and burning.

4. When sago turns transparent, pour into a sieve and wash under cold running water to remove excess starch. Place into individual moulds or small bowls and leave to cool and set. Refrigerate when cooled.

5. Prepare gula melaka syrup by boiling in water with pandan leaves for 15 minutes until thickened. Strain and set aside.

6. Empty tinned coconut milk into a serving jug and stir to mix evenly.

5. To serve, run a knife round the mould or bowl to release the sago and tip over a shallow dish. Top with coconut milk and palm sugar syrup.

INGREDIENTS

$^1/_2$ oz (12g) agar agar powder
4 fl oz (120ml) cold water
$1^3/_4$ pints (1litre) boiling water
8oz (225g) sugar
3 pandan leaves
4oz (110g) coconut powder dissolved in
2oz (55ml) hot water

SERVES

4-6

PREPARATION

20 minutes

INGREDIENTS

1 cup pearl sago, soaked and rinsed
1 cup granulated sugar
4 cups water
$1^1/_2$ cups grated coconut, dark skin removed
1 tbsp caster sugar pinch of salt
drop of red food colouring
pinch of salt

SERVES

4-6

PREPARATION

30 minutes

AGAR AGAR

Nonya jelly.

METHOD

1. Dissolve sugar in boiling water. Run a fork through the pandan leaves and tie them into a knot. Add to the boiling sugar and simmer for 5 minutes to release the fragrance.

2. Dissolve agar agar powder in cold water and pour boiling syrup over it. Simmer for 10 minutes. Divide agar agar syrup into 2 portions, pour half into a 7in diameter flan dish or mould to set.

3. Continue simmering the remaining half of the agar agar syrup for a further 10 minutes to reduce. Add coconut cream and stir to mix evenly.

4. Ensure that the first layer of coloured agar agar has almost set before pouring in the coconut flavoured layer. Leave to cool and refrigerate. Remove from mould and serve or cut into cubes (see picture opposite).

COCONUT SAGO

Nonya sago pudding.

METHOD

1. Dissolve the sugar and water in a saucepan and bring to the boil. Add sago and stir constantly over low heat for 10 minutes until the sago is transparent.

2. Add red food colouring and stir to mix evenly. Pour cooked sago into a shallow dish and leave to cool. Refrigerate when cooled.

3. Add a pinch of salt and caster sugar to the grated coconut. Mix well. When the sago has cooled down and set, cut them up into neat 1in cubes and roll to coat each piece in the grated coconut. Return to the refrigerator to chill before serving.

The gelatinous texture of Agar agar, a natural seaweed, takes some getting used to. It is however very refreshing after a meal and is enjoyed by Southeast Asians who also value its 'cooling' properties. Enriched with coconut cream, it can be quite delicious..

INGREDIENTS

8 oz (225g) yam, peeled and diced into $\frac{1}{2}$in cubes

8 oz(225g) sweet potato, peeled and diced into $\frac{1}{2}$in cubes

4oz (110g) pearl sago, soaked for 20 minutes and rinsed

1 pint water

8oz (225g) sugar

8oz (225g) coconut powder dissolved in 1 cup hot water

3 pandan leaves

SERVES

6-8

PREPARATION

30 minutes

BUBUR CHA CHA

Southeast Asians are fond of coconut based puddings in all forms. They do not necessarily eat them directly after a meal as Europeans do but perhaps an hour or two later when the main meal has been more or less digested. The original recipe for Bubur cha cha includes multicoloured chewy sago bits which, although it does not have a distinctive taste, makes a contrasting impact on the pudding with its texture and rainbow colours. As kids, we had fun helping to make these coloured sago bits and watching them deepen in colour as they rose to the top when dropped into boiling water. Of course, the biggest enjoyment was in devouring the end product which is a favourite for all of us. For the sake of simplicity, I have substituted pearl sago balls.

METHOD

1. Boil the yam and sweet potato in a saucepan with the water. Run a fork through the pandan leaves to release the flavour and tie into a knot. Add to the boiling yams.

2. Simmer for 15 minutes and add sago. Stir and simmer for a few more minutes until the sago has turned transparent.

3. Sweeten with palm sugar and add coconut milk. Cook over low heat so as not to curdle the coconut. Serve hot in individual bowls.

INGREDIENTS
1lb 2oz (500 g) glutinous rice, soaked for 2 hours
8oz (225ml) tinned coconut milk

COCONUT CUSTARD
6 eggs, lightly beaten
16oz (450g) coconut milk
1 cup sugar
3oz (75g) plain flour
$\frac{1}{2}$ tsp vanilla essence
10 pandan leaves, chopped

SERVES
6-8

PREPARATION
60 minutes

PULOT SERIKAYA
Steamed glutinous rice with coconut custard.

Pandan leaves have a beautiful vanilla-like fragrance and are often used in puddings and desserts for that reason. They also contain a natural colouring and the combination of the two makes them a prized ingredient. In the tropical heat, they are often grown in the backgarden as a handy standby but the attractive green foliage is another reason for its prolific domestic cultivation.
If you are unable to get hold of pandan leaves, substitute green colouring and use vanilla essence.

METHOD
1. Rinse and drain the soaked glutinous rice. Spread on a heat resistant dish (9in diameter and 3in deep) and mix with coconut milk. Steam for 30 minutes until rice is cooked. Leave to cool.

2. Put chopped pandan leaves into a liquidiser with 1 cup water and blend for a minute or two. Put through strainer and squeeze to extract the green juice.

3. Combine pandan extract with the remaining custard ingredients and mix well in a liquidiser.

4. Gently stir custard over a double boiler until it starts to thicken.

5. When rice is sufficiently cool to handle, press down to compress and pour slightly thickened custard mixture over the top. Return to the steamer and cook gently for 4-5 minutes.

6. Remove from steamer when cooked and leave to cool. Serve at room temperature. Do not refrigerate as the rice will harden.

Best eaten on the day.

INGREDIENTS
16oz (450g) can lychees
8oz (225g) caster sugar
10 fl oz (285ml) plain unsweetened yogurt
10 fl oz (285ml) double cream, lightly whipped

SERVES
4-6

PREPARATION
30 minutes

LYCHEE ICE CREAM

Nothing tastes better than homemade ice cream and it is not as difficult to make as one might suppose.

METHOD

1. Strain the lychees and put the syrup in a saucepan with the sugar. Chop the lychees in a liquidiser or food processor and add these to the pan and boil for 15 minutes to make a syrup. Allow to cool.

2. Whip the cream and yogurt until it stands in peaks and fold in the cooled lychee syrup.

3. Put into the ice cream maker to churn. Alternatively, put into a rigid container and freeze for 2 hours, stirring after every hour to break up the ice crystals. If you have a hand-held electric beater, introduce this straight into the container and beat for a minute or two. Freeze until solid. Serve decorated with whole lychees.

INGREDIENTS
2 ripe mango
8oz (225g) caster sugar
10 fl oz (285ml) plain unsweetened yogurt
10 fl oz (285ml) thick double cream

GARNISH
Fresh mango slices or raspberries
Sprig of mint

SERVES
4-6

PREPARATION
30 minutes

MANGO ICE CREAM

You will need full flavoured overripe mangoes for this recipe, the ideal way of using mangoes that are too soft to be served cut.

METHOD

1. Peel and pare the mangoes. Puree with the caster sugar in a food processor.

2. Lightly whip yogurt with double cream until it stands in peaks.

3. Fold mango puree into the whipped cream and yogurt and pour into an ice cream maker. Alternatively pour into a rigid container and freeze for 2 hours, stirring at the end of each hour to break up any ice crystals. An electric hand beater is ideal for this purpose.

4. Freeze until solid. Serve garnished with fresh mango slices or raspberries and a sprig of mint for contrasting colour.

Dips and Sauces

SAMBAL NANAS

SAMBAL TIMUN

SATAY SAUCE

PICKLED GREEN CHILLIES

SERUNDING

SAMBAL MANGA

SAMBAL BLACHAN

CHILLI AND GARLIC SAUCE

CHILLI AND GINGER SAUCE

SWEET CHILLI SAUCE

BAWANG GORENG

CHILLI PADI SAUCE

It is rare for a Southeast Asian meal not to include a dipping sauce, condiment or pickle to enhance the meal. Noodles are always served with a plateful of freshly sliced chillies in light soya and pickles are eaten to cut through greasy fried dishes and serves as a relish.

It is important to mention that the particular varieties of sauces and dips are also carefully chosen to complement each dish and are seldom eaten at random and mismatched. I suppose it is one of those things that stem from habit and tradition in the same way mint is served with lamb and horseradish with beef. Various types of chilli sauces abound and each variation meant for a particular dish. I found it disconcerting to see European diners in my restaurants dipping their prawn wantuns into satay sauce and satay into sweet chilli and garlic sauce.

INGREDIENTS

1 cucumber, deseeded
$1/_2$ pineapple, cut into pieces (or use 16 oz tinned)
2 dsp vinegar
$1/_2$ tsp salt, to taste
1 dsp dark soya sauce
1 tbsp sambal blachan (see page 134)

SAMBAL NANAS

Pineapple and cucumber salad in sambal blachan dressing.
This is a typical Nonya salad with sambal blachan dressing that is served as a condiment to rich coconut based curries or greasy fried noodles to refresh the palate.
I was always a fussy eater and my mother used to rack her brains to cook something that would make me eat. This is one of my favourites and is enough to lead me to the table without further coaxing.

METHOD

1. Cut the cucumber along its length into quarters. Remove the the seeds and chop the cucumber into cubes.

2. Combine the cucumber and pineapple pieces with the sambal blachan, vinegar, sugar and salt and toss to mix.

SAMBAL TIMUN

Dried prawn and cucumber salad in sambal blachan dressing.

Similar to the pineapple and cucumber salad, this Nonya salad is a refreshing side salad enriched with dried prawns which makes it rather potent. A must at weddings and feasts. The dried prawns may be offensive to the Western palate, but are greatly appreciated by the connoisseur.

INGREDIENTS

1 cucumber
1 cup dried prawns
2 shallots, finely sliced
1 tbsp sambal blachan
2 dsp sugar
$1/_2$ tsp salt
1 dsp lime juice
1 tsp vinegar

METHOD

1. Cut the cucumber along its length into 4 long strips. Remove seeds and then slice at an angle into $1/_2$in thick slices.

2. Soak dried prawns in 1 cup boiling water for 20 minutes to soften. Drain and roughly chop in food processor.

3. Combine cucumber, shallots and dried prawns with dressing ingredients and toss.

INGREDIENTS

*1lb (450g) roasted peanuts, chopped in food
processor
3 tbsp sugar
1 tsp salt
4oz (110g) coconut powder dissolved in 1 cup
hot water
1 pint (570ml) water
3 dsp cooking oil*

REMPAH

*20 dried chillies, soaked in hot water to soften
3 stalks lemon grass, finely sliced
1in galanggal, finely sliced
1 large onion, finely chopped
2 cloves garlic, finely sliced
6 candlenuts
2 tbsp cooking oil*

GROUND SPICES:

*$^1/_2$ tsp ground black pepper
1 tbsp ground coriander,
1 tsp ground fennel
1 tsp ground cumin
$^1/_2$ tsp turmeric
1 tbsp chilli powder*

INGREDIENTS

*6oz (175g) large green chillies
2 tsp salt
1 dsp sugar
10 floz (275ml) malt vinegar*

S A T A Y   S A U C E

A spicy peanut sauce to be served with Satay.

METHOD

1. Blend rempah in liquidiser until fine.

2. Heat oil in wok and fry rempah until fragrant, stirring constantly to prevent sticking and burning.

3. Add coconut milk, sugar and ground spices. Mix evenly.

4. Bring to the boil and add chopped nuts. Stir to mix and top up with water.

5. Simmer for another 5 minutes and keep hot. Serve with satay.

The sauce will thicken with time as the nuts absorb all the liquid. To re-use, top up with a little more water to dilute. The sauce will keep for up to a week refrigerated or frozen. As it is labour intensive, it is best to make up a large batch and freeze in smaller quantities for each occasion satay is served.

P I C K L E D   G R E E N   C H I L L I E S

These are normally served with Cantonese style noodles. Pickling also reduces the pungency but the larger green chillies are not as ferocious as the red ones.

METHOD

Remove the stalks of the green chillies and slice them into $^1/_2$in or $^1/_4$in rings all the way down to the tip. Put into a clean jar and mix with sugar, salt and malt vinegar. Leave overnight before using. Will keep for several weeks without being refrigerated.

INGREDIENTS

8oz (225g) desiccated coconut
8oz (225g) tinned coconut milk
4 tbsp cooking oil
1 tbsp coriander powder
1 tsp fennel powder
1 tbsp sugar
4 lime leaves, finely sliced
1 tsp salt
1 dsp tamarind, soaked in $^1/_2$ cup water to extract juice

REMPAH

15 dried chillies, soaked in 1 cup hot water
2 lemon grass, finely sliced
$^1/_2$ in galanggal, finely sliced
1 in fresh turmeric, or 1 tsp ground
3 cloves garlic
4 shallots
2 tbsp cooking oil

INGREDIENTS

2 medium green mangoes
1 dsp sambal blachan
1 dsp sugar
$^1/_2$ tsp salt

SERUNDING

A spicy coconut condiment served with pressed rice cakes and a vegetable stew in coconut milk.

For maximum flavour, freshly desiccated coconut should be used to make this dish but I have made it with dried desiccated coconut. I have always felt that the commercially marketed dried desiccated coconut is in fact the chaff that remains after the coconut cream has been extracted because there is hardly any creaminess left in them when they are reconstituted with water. I have therefore added tinned coconut milk to supplement the coconut flavour.

METHOD

1. Blend the rempah in a liquidiser until fine.

2. Heat 4 tbsp cooking oil in a wok or saucepan and fry the rempah until fragrant and the oil starts to separate from the mix. Add the powdered spices, and season with salt, sugar and tamarind juice.

3. Add dry roasted coconut, coconut milk and lime leaves and fry until all the liquid has evaporated.

Leave to cool before serving.

SAMBAL MANGA

Mango salad with sambal blachan.

METHOD

Peel the skin off the mangoes and either grate the flesh on a stainless steel grater or pare right down to the stone and chop finely. Put chopped mango pieces, salt, sugar and sambal blachan into a mini processor and blend for no more than 10 seconds. The idea is to blend the mango pieces with the sambal without actually grinding it into a paste. Serve as a relish for fried fish with plain rice.

INGREDIENTS

10 large red chillies, deseeded if wished
a piece of blachan 2 x 2 x $^1/_2$ in roasted
$^1/_2$ tsp salt

S A M B A L   B L A C H A N

This is a chilli condiment that can be eaten either as a chilli dip or combined with other ingredients for a salad or dressing.

The dried prawn paste (blachan) must be roasted and this is can be done either over an open fire or roasted in an oven. Cook till the pieces have formed a dark brown crust. If you are roasting them in the oven, wrap the blachan pieces in foil to contain the smells. Open kitchen windows and doors to air and close all interior doors to bedrooms and sitting room. The resulting odours can be very offensive and tend to linger.

METHOD

Thinly slice red chillies and blend in mini food processor with blachan and salt to a fine paste. Serve with a squeeze of lime juice as a condiment or chilli dip.

INGREDIENTS

8 large red chillies, finely sliced
4 cloves fresh garlic, finely sliced
1 dsp sugar
1 tsp salt
1 dsp vinegar or lime juice

C H I L L I   A N D   G A R L I C   S A U C E

A delicious chilli dip for fried foods and sauce for noodles.

METHOD

Combine all ingredients in a mini food processor and pulse until the chillies are finely chopped into a paste.

INGREDIENTS

8 large red chillies, finely sliced
4 cloves garlic, finely sliced
$^1/_2$ in fresh ginger, finely sliced
1 tsp sugar
1 tsp salt
1 dsp fish sauce
1 dsp vinegar

C H I L L I   A N D   G I N G E R   S A U C E

This is the chilli sauce normally served with Hainanese chicken rice.

METHOD

Combine all ingredients in a mini food processor or liquidiser and pulse until fine.

Keeps for up to a week in a covered jar in the refrigerator.

INGREDIENTS
8 large red chillies, finely sliced
4 cloves garlic, finely sliced
6 oz pineapple pieces (tinned) and juices
1 tbsp brown sugar
1 tsp salt
2 dsp fish sauce
1 dsp vinegar

SWEET CHILLI SAUCE
Delicious served with fried food and starter dips..

METHOD
Combine all ingredients in a mini food processor and pulse until fine. Simmer in a heavy saucepan on gentle heat for 30 minutes, stirring every now and then to prevent sticking and burning.

A universal sauce and certainly the one I use the most. Keeps for several days in a covered jar in the refrigerator.

INGREDIENTS
10-12 oriental shallots
(or use 1 medium onion, finely chopped)
1 cup cooking oil for frying

BAWANG GORENG
Crispy fried onion rings.

METHOD
Peel the shallots and slice finely and evenly across the grain. Heat the cooking oil in a wok until it starts to smoke and fry the shallots for 2-3 minutes until golden brown and crisp. Transfer with a slotted spoon and drain on paper towels. Store in an airtight container if not used immediately and they should remain crisp for several weeks.

INGREDIENTS
$1/2$ cup bird's eye chillies (Chilli padi)
$1/2$ tsp salt
$1/2$ tsp sugar

CHILLI PADI SAUCE

METHOD
Remove stalks from chillies and place in a mini food processor with salt and sugar. Pulse until the chillies are finely chopped, stopping the motor every now and then to rearrange the chillies so that they fall into the blades.

Mix chopped chillies with oil leftover from frying the rempah.

GLOSSARY OF INGREDIENTS

AGAR AGAR

A gelatin processed from seaweed which sets without refrigeration. Used mainly as a dessert in southeast Asian cuisines, generally sweetened with sugar, enriched with coconut cream and set in pretty moulds. Agar agar is sold in almost all oriental supermarkets in dried strands resembling white rafia, or in powdered form. The powdered form tends to have added colouring.

ASIAN BASIL

Not dissimilar to Italian basil but more pungent. Used very widely in Thai cooking, stirfried into chicken and seafood dishes, served fresh as a garnish, tossed into salads and wrapped round spring rolls with lettuce. It has small green leaves, darker than the Italian variety, and purple flowers and a strong anisette aroma. Available mostly in Thai and Vietnamese supermarkets. Will last only a few days in the refrigerator before the leaves start to blacken at the edges and dry out.

ANISE, STAR

It is very easy to identify this eight-pointed pod amongst all the spices. It is one of the few spices used in Chinese cooking and is a component of the five-spice powder. Tends to be used whole, especially in soups and for braising meat like pork in soya sauce. It will keep indefinitely.

BAMBOO SHOOTS

Although fresh bamboo shoots are sometimes available in Chinese supermarkets, it is just as good to use the canned version as it has already been boiled and tenderised. However, there is often a strong undesirable smell in some brands of canned bamboo shoots. This can be overcome by boiling again in fresh water for a few minutes and draining. Canned bamboo shoots come as whole shoots, or ready cut into julienne strips or thin slices. Picking the right one for the recipe you are using saves labour. They are ideal for adding to stir-fried vegetables as the crunchy texture livens up the dish. Any unused shoots can be stored in water in the refrigerator for up to 2 weeks, although you will need to change the water every other day.

BEANCURD

Also known as Tofu or Tauhu, is a byproduct of soya beans, this is made from cooked soya beans, pureed and strained to produce soya milk which is then set into milky white curd with the help of nigari (magnesium chloride). Preserved for longer shelf life, beancurd is now available in the larger supermarkets, health food shops as well as oriental emporiums. Fresh beancurd is always sold packed in water and vacuum packing has prolonged the shelf life by up to a week or more.

It does not have a particularly strong taste but is high in protein, hence is ideal for vegetarians. Once you get used to the soft wheylike texture, it can be quite delicious especially if cooked in the various different ways that have developed in Thai, Nonya, Indonesian and even Malay cuisines. In Singapore, beancurd comes in two textures, soft (tauhu) for adding to soups, and the firmer and easier to handle taukwa which can be used for braising and deepfrying.

Ready-fried beancurd called Tauhu Pok is also found in Chinese supermarkets. The hollowed centre is ideal for stuffing with marinated minced pork or blanched beansprouts and julienned cucumber, to be eaten drizzled with a dressing.

In Singapore and Malaysia, this dressing is normally made from a heady prawn paste called heyko combined with sugar and chillies and chopped nuts - utterly delicious to the locals but perhaps an acquired taste for foreigners who will find the aroma of heyko similar to that of blachan. Tauhu pok can also be used to add to stirfried dishes, and goes particularly well with beansprouts and spring onions, cooked for just a few seconds to retain the crispness.

BEANS, LONG

Available only from Southeast Asian supermarkets at present, these legumes grow to about 1-2 feet in length, although some varieties are even longer, hence they are also known as yard beans.

Those available here tend to be stringier than the ones I used to eat as a child and I have therefore refrained from paying the extra to cook them in this country, substituting kenyan beans or string beans. Long beans retain their shape in braising and stews and keep well in the refrigerator.

BLACHAN

A malodorous paste made from dried salted shrimps. Usually comes in a block and is sold only in oriental supermarkets.

Westerners would find it difficult to come to terms with the smell as it is not dissimilar from rotting flesh and cooking with it tends to pervade the atmosphere. My advice would be to use it in very small quantities until you get used to it and have developed a taste for it as most Nonya and Malay recipes call for its use. Keep the kitchen door closed as well as the doors to other rooms and ventilate all rooms afterwards. An excellent antidote to counteract the unpleasant odours apart from air fresheners would be to boil some pandan leaves in a saucepan and allow the beautiful fragrance to naturally vaporise into the air.

High in protein, blachan gives much depth to Malaysian and Nonya curries, normally termed sambals. The difficulty arises when a vegetarian dish is cooked with sambal sauce as the prawn content would automatically disqualify the dish for vegans. In Malaysia I was told they have developed vegetarian blachan from a certain fruit but I have not as yet discovered the source.

Highly preserved, blachan has an indefinite shelf life and does not need to be kept refrigerated but I would recommend storing it in a cool place, rewrapped after opening with several layers of cling film or foil, and then placed in a tight fitting jar or plastic box.

CANDLENUTS

Also known as Kemiri Nuts or Buah Keras, is the size of a hazelnut in its shell. Candlenuts are widely used in Malay, Indonesian and Nonya recipes (unknown north of the Peninsular) to thicken sauces and as a substitute for coconut cream. They have a waxy appearance and in days of old, were used to make candles. Cannot be eaten raw as they have an unpleasant bitter taste and toxic properties unless cooked beforehand. They are available in Chinese supermarkets. They can be replaced by almonds, brazil nuts, cashew nuts or macadamia nuts, although these are more expensive.

If kept unrefrigerated for any length of time, they will develop larvae but some shops sell them vacuum packed which prolongs their shelf life. Can also be kept frozen.

They should be ground in a food processor before blending with other spice ingredients in a liquidiser so as not to cause damage to the blades and motor of your liquidiser.

CARDAMON

More commonly used in Indian cooking, several varieties of cardamon exist. The tiny black seeds within the white husky pod are powerfully aromatic and the pods should be crushed before use to release the flavour. The Indian influence to the cuisines of southeast Asia is clearly evidenced in the widespread use of this spice in the curries and rice dishes of Indonesia and Nonya and Malay cuisines. Will keep indefinitely.

CASSIA BARK

is very often mistaken for cinnamon as its flavour is so similar to the more superior spice but considerably cheaper. Sometimes referred to as Chinese cinnamon as it is native to Hunan in China whereas cinnamon comes from Sri Lanka.

Added to braising meats and soups in stick form, as well as a flavouring for rice and curries.

CHILLIES

were first introduced to the cuisines of Europe and Asia by Columbus who brought them back from their native land Brazil. Today, chillies play a fundamental part in the cuisines of Southeast Asia especially. Several hybrid varieties have evolved with time and local conditions ranging from the miniscule Thai variety which despite its size is volcanic in pungency, to the fatter and rounder African types. In principle, the smaller and thinner varieties are more potent than the fat round ones. Their colours, red, green or even yellow, are also no indication of the degree of pungency.

Ironically, chillies are appropriate for consuming in hot climates as they stimulate the appetite and the nerves, blood circulation and perspiration thus combating the lethargy and stagnation of hot weather. However, it is unlikely that one would eat chillies merely for clinical reasons and suffer the powerful consequences.

It is best to determine the strength of the particular variety before adding liberally to one's dishes by tasting a tiny slice. Removing the tiny white seeds within the pod will reduce its potency.

GLOSSARY OF INGREDIENTS

Chillies are best kept refrigerated where they will last for several weeks. Removing the stalks which tend to rot first, will help to prolong their life. They can also be left to dry out naturally or they can be pickled in a saline and vinegar solution. Whole chillies should not be frozen as they tend to go mushy when defrosted but there is no reason why they should be frozen in a pureed form.

CHINESE DRIED MUSHROOMS

These are shitake mushrooms which have been dried. The caps are dark brown or black and range from 13 inches in diameter. The quality determines the price although those from Japan are

even more expensive than their Chinese counterparts. To reconstitute, soak in a bowl of boiling water for at least 20 minutes. The soaking liquid can be reserved for adding to the dish if more liquid is called for. If the mushrooms come with stems, these are best removed as they are so hard as to be inedible even after cooking. Although in their dried form they should keep indefinitely, they suffer from larvae infection and should be checked regulaly. Alternatively, store in a deep freeze.

C H I V E S ,   C H I N E S E

Much stronger than European chives. They grow to about a foot in length and are therefore much thicker and longer than European chives, resembling blades of grass. Used in Chinese dim sum preparations and go well with stirfried beansprouts. Singaporeans serve them sprinkled over Mee siam, a spicy tamarind based noodle dish with Thai origins and a favourite hawker stall dish.

C O C O N U T

One of the reasons why it is irksome to cook some Southeast Asian dishes outside of Southeast Asia is the lack of fresh desiccated coconut which one merely picks up from the market along with the rest of the shopping. The coconut seller has a pile of fresh coconut which he pops into a grinder and out comes freshly grated coconut ready for use. For a long time the only source of fresh coconut was the occasional sighting in a large London supermarket chain which one would have to crack open, prise out the flesh, remove the brown skin and then either grate manually on a metal grater, or chop into small bits and put through a liquidiser. This laborious, and sometimes even hazardous, procedure usually leads one to resort to the creamed coconut blocks available, which is far inferior to the real McCoy as these coconut blocks tend to smell of rancid oil. However, more recently tinned coconut milk from Thailand became available. More recently still, packets of coconut powder made by Nestlé and other brands appeared on the supermarket shelves and these I have found to be quite acceptable for cooking purposes. Dissolved in hot water, instant coconut cream is now used even in Southeast Asia, especially in catering establishments because squeezing coconut milk from grated coconuts can be a chore when large quantities are required. For busy cooks, having instant

coconut powder in the larder makes a lot of sense.

For those who still prefer freshly squeezed coconut milk, this is what you do:

To crack open the hard shell, first wrap the coconut in cling film, hold the coconut with one hand over a sink, hit down the middle with the back (blunt end) of a heavy cleaver with a few sharp knocks until it cracks and splits open, releasing a clear white liquid (coconut water), and exposing the white flesh inside. The reason for the cling film is to contain any splinters and husks, and of course the coconut water. Continue hitting the shell until the coconut is sufficiently broken to enable you to get at the kernel. Remove cling film and drain the water,

Make an insertion into the white flesh and then prise out segments close to the cut. When you have finally managed to remove all the flesh, rinse under a cold tap. Chop into even smaller bits and put them into a liquidiser with 2 cups of warm water. Liquidise until the water is completely absorbed by the coconut. Strain through calico bag or a clean kitchen cloth or teatowel, squeezing hard to extract as much milk as possible until the coconut feels dry. To obtain a second extraction, return the desiccated coconut to the liquidiser with 2 more cups of warm water and pulse for a few seconds. Repeat the straining and squeezing procedure into a separate container as the second extraction would obviously produce a thinner milk which is used in certain recipes. The whole process takes half an hour or more and can be very messy.

Cream of coconut can be obtained by allowing the first extraction to sit and creaming off the top layer which rises. The liquid which settles at the bottom may be used as thin coconut milk or discarded.

As a rule, fresh coconut milk is only necessary for desserts and sweets, especially in Sago melaka or Chendol, where the flavour of the coconut determines the quality of the dessert. There have been occasions when I have had to resort to fresh cream or milk as a substitute and remarkably, no one has noticed the difference.

C O R I A N D E R ,
F R E S H

When a recipe calls for fresh coriander, it normally refers to fresh coriander leaves as opposed to seeds or powder, which imparts

GLOSSARY OF INGREDIENTS

an entirely different flavour to the dish. Fresh coriander leaves are widely available and are now available in small sachets in supermarkets. They are however much cheaper by the bunch in oriental supermarkets as these usually come with roots. Stand them in a jug of water and they will last much longer. They are also relatively easy to grow from seed. Coriander leaves are best served roughly chopped and added to salads and sprinkled over soups, curries and many dishes as a garnish.

The Thais use the roots and stem of the coriander plant in their curry pastes. The juice extracted from pounding the roots is also added to salad dressings and marinades, giving an exquisite aromatic flavour.

CORIANDER SEEDS

In Southeast Asian cuisines, coriander seeds are usually ground into powder. Check through for stones and foreign bodies before use. Dryfrying them in a skillet or frying pan or roasting in the oven just before use releases their aromatic oils and improves their flavour. Use a coffee grinder as required.

CUMIN SEEDS

This is a spice normally associated with Indian and Middle Eastern cooking. Now grown in the hot tropical countries of north Africa, the Middle East, India and the Americas, where the Spanish use it to flavour rice, sausages and stuffed vegetables. The thin light brown grains are often mistaken for fennel seeds and vice versa. It has an unmistakable sweet fragrance which is heightened by toasting. Best stored in its seed form as ground cumin loses its flavour much quicker.

CURRY LEAVES

As the name suggests, curry leaves are in the main used in Indian curry dishes, principally south India. The immigrant southern Indians therefore brought this herb with them to Malaysia and Singapore where they are cultivated in the back gardens along with all the other local herbs. Not grown commercially they can be difficult to find. Sold only in Indian supermarkets, you may have to make a special trip to areas like Southall, Tooting, Brick Lane and any Indian enclaves. Malaysian and Singaporean Indians do insist upon their use to improve the flavour of their curries.

Added to stirfried thinly sliced white cabbage with mustard seeds, it makes this ordinary vegetable into an exotic delicacy. An essential ingredient in southern Indian pickles, vegetables and fish dishes. The fresh leaves can be left to dry naturally and then stored in an air tight jar or frozen.

CURRY POWDER

is a combination of spices in measured proportions premixed to facilitate the cooking of a curry dish. The spices are then mixed with water to form a paste and added to the other ingredients of pounded onions, ginger and garlic, whole spices of cloves, cinnamon sticks and star anise, and of course the meat or vegetables. For fish curries, tamarind is always added to remove the 'fishy' flavour as well as giving it a sour taste which complements fish, just as lemon juice is added to fish dishes in European recipes. The southern Indians also like to add coconut cream to thicken and enrich their curries whereas northern Indians use yogurt.

There are obviously hundreds of recipes in varying quantities as devised by each family and chef but the basic ingredients tend to remain the same. Some families however prefer to mix their spices as they cook but I feel that this is not only timewasting considering the number of spices that go to make a curry, it can also be difficult to duplicate the exact recipe each time.

Commercial preparations available in Europe can be very disappointing and very often are not sufficiently authentic unless you know the particular brand to go for. In Singapore and Malaysia, the locals actually seek out the little Indian shops and mills with their own mixture where they can be certain that the ingredients used are fresh and the recipe is liked. I go to the extent of having mine flown in from Kuala Lumpur, Malaysia where my friend Mrs Saro Velu knows exactly which shop to buy from. It is a pity they do not export this particular mixture to all the supermarkets in Europe - you could all be cooking delicious authentic curries every time.

Here are a few recipes for you to try mixing your own. Store in an airtight glass jar. Use 2-3 dessertspoonfuls of the curry powder for each 1lb of meat and follow the recipe for the individual styles of curries. You should always mix the curry powder with a little water into a wet paste first before cooking as the dry powdered mixture burns very easily. As mentioned

earlier in my note under curry leaves, the use of these accentuates the flavour even further.

MEAT CURRY POWDER

(for chicken, lamb, or beef)
500g ground coriander; 150g ground fennel; 100g ground cumin; 200g ground chillies; 50g ground black pepper; 60g ground turmeric; 20 g ground cinnamon; 10 g ground cardamon; 10 g ground cloves

FISH CURRY POWDER

1kg coriander seeds; 200g fennel powder; 200g cumin powder; 200g chilli powder; 100g ground black pepper; 100g ground turmeric; 20g cardamon pods (remove outer husk and crush seeds finely); 10g star anise and 10g cloves (finely ground); 1tsp cinnamon powder ; 20g fenugreek seeds, finely ground.

If using whole seeds, dry roast for 10-15 minutes before grinding in coffee mill.

D AUN KESO M

Also known as Laksa leaves or Vietnamese mint. Strange as it may seem, this herb is fairly unknown in Thailand whereas the Vietnamese eat them fresh, amongst the many fresh herbs like mint, dill and coriander, and sprinkled over soups. In Singapore they are more commonly served fresh with laksa and although only a few leaves are served over the bowl of this deliciously spicy coconut noodle soup the dish seems incomplete without it. They are not as yet available in the west, perhaps due to the lack of demand or because they do not travel well, wilting within hours of harvest.

D RIED SHRIMP S

These have been salted and dried and used extensively in all southeast Asian cuisines. They are used to add extra flavour to the dishes but are not always liked by everyone. They have their own distinctive taste and I tend to use them only in certain recipes where I feel they will not conflict but rather complement the other ingredients used. However, in the Nonya dish of Sambal udang Kering (Dried Prawn Sambal), they are transformed into a dish in their own right with the combination of chillies, candlenuts, onions and prawn paste. Served as a side dish, condiment or appetiser, it can even be a sandwich filling.

F ENNEL SEED S

Like cumin seeds, these resemble brown rice grains but fennel seeds are slightly larger and lighter in colour. Some even have greenish tints. They have the flavour of aniseed, and are one of the ingredients in curry mixtures. Chinese recipes use them whole, stuffed in roast duck and to flavour soups.

F ENUGREE K

A spice associated with Indian cooking, fenugreek has western origins and derived its name from the Latin for 'Greek hay' when the plant was used as animal fodder. It is also renowned for its healing qualities and is used in medicinal preparations for lowering blood pressure, oral contraceptives and veterinary medications.

The small golden yellow seeds are usually available in Indian stores. Apart from being one of the ingredients in curry powders, fenugreek is also used in vegetable dishes and accentuates fish dishes. Only very small quantities of it are required to flavour a dish.

F ISH SAUC E

Is a fundamental seasoning in Burmese, Thai and Vietnamese cuisines. Known as nam pla in Thailand and nuoc mam in Vietnam, it is made from fermenting heavily salted anchovies under the hot tropical sun. The thin light brown liquid is strained and bottled. It does not need refrigeration even after opening although it is best kept in a cool place. Keeps indefinitely due to its high salt content. Large salt crystals which settle at the bottom are sometimes mistaken for broken glass. This seasoning is equivalent to adding a flavour enhancer and can be used with seafood, vegetables and meats. Its fishy smell dissipates with cooking. Also delicious as a dipping sauce for fried fish or chicken, especially when mixed with lime or lemon juice and slices of fresh chillies.

F I V E S P I C E   P O W D E R

The aromatic Chinese blend of spices comprising star anise, fennel or anise seeds, cloves, cinammon and Szechuan peppercorns. It is used to season meat and poultry, particularly for roasting and is available in all oriental grocery stores.

G A L A N G G A L

Also known as lengkuas, galanggal is another rhizome related to the ginger family. Its skin is more opaque with a pinkish tinge. Unlike ginger however, it has a fiery medicinal and bitter taste and is not palatable raw but its flavour is best released in cooking when combined with other ingredients like garlic, lemon grass and chillies. Like the ginger, it has the ability to curb nausea and aids digestion. A tonic is made from grated galanggal and lime juice.

Cut across the grain when using galanggal as the tissues are very fibrous. It can be frozen but I would recommend slicing it first as the juices in the root turn to ice in the freezing process and are lost when thawed out, leaving the fibres. Lasts for a week or so in the vegetable compartment in the refrigerator. In rempah making, is almost always used with lemon grass as they complement one another.

G A L A N G G A L   L E S S E R

Another rhizome related to ginger, it is sometimes known as aromatic ginger, Krachai or Kenchur. Not as widely used as the other rhizomes it can be omitted from the recipes if unavailable. However, it does add a more pronounced flavour to the dishes. It comes in clusters of brown fingers about 2-3in in length. The plant is native to southern China and used by the Chinese in a medicinal capacity. Dried and powdered kenchur is available for adding to curry pastes and rempahs if fresh ones are not available. Follow freezing instructions as for galanggal above.

G A R A M   M A S A L A

A mixture of ground spices for use in curries and Indian cooking.

G A R L I C

Indigenous to Asia, garlic has been used as food and medicine from time immemorial. Its curative powers are wide ranging, for coughs, colds, bronchitis and high blood pressure, asthma, skin problems and boils. It has the ability not only to destroy diseases but also to prevent infection and is effective as an external antiseptic, not to mention its legendary powers in warding off evil spirits and vampires.

Its culinary uses are universal. In Southeast Asian dishes, it is hard to find a recipe that does not contain garlic. Surprisingly, given the amount of garlic that is consumed by everyone, the people of southeast Asia do not seem to suffer from excessive personal odours.

Choose bulbs that are heavy to ensure that they are fresh. They can be kept without refrigeration and very often make decorative hangings in the kitchen. Dried garlic flakes are now available in Chinese supermarkets and widely used in catering establishments where large quantities are required. To reconstitute, soak in warm water for 10 minutes. It has a slightly musty flavour in this form and is therefore not recommended for use when garlic is used in its uncooked state as in salad dressings or some fresh chilli sauces.

G I N G E R

A tropical plant, the root (rhizome) is highly prized as a culinary ingredient and used extensively in Asian cuisines. Like garlic, it too has numerous extraordinary curative properties. It is thought to aid digestion, combat colds and stimulate the appetite. A pregnant Chinese woman eats massive amounts of ginger to alleviate nausea and her diet during this period of confinement is at least one pound of ginger a day sliced finely and stir fried with livers, pork and braised with chicken. It is considered a 'heaty' food and combined with sesame oil (also heaty), fortifies the woman in time for labour when her pores would be opened in childbirth.

Ginger has cleansing properties. It suppresses any hint of rankness in meat and fish and therefore refreshes the dish. A few slices added to boiling stock not only gives it extra flavour, it cuts out any unpleasant odours.

When buying ginger, choose heavy pieces with taut skin. When they have been left to sit around for too long, the skins wrinkle up and the flesh becomes more fibrous. This makes slicing more difficult. Ginger is also available in many forms, dried, powdered, preserved with syrup and crystallized with sugar, for use in both savoury and sweet dishes, cakes, biscuits and pastries.

H E Y K O

Concentrated preserved prawn paste. Resembles thick treacle but has a strong smell because of its composition. Used mainly in Singapore, Malaysia and Indonesia in a salad called Rojak where it is made into a dressing with sugar, chopped peanuts and chillies and eaten with tart fruits, yam bean, blanched beansprouts and cucumber among other salad ingredients. The same dressing is used in stuffed fried beancurd. An acquired taste. Available in 14oz plastic tubs in Chinese supermarkets.

H O I S I N   S A U C E

is a thick reddish brown sauce made from soybean paste, garlic, sugar and a touch of spice. Usually served with Peking or Aromatic Duck. It can also be used as a base for barbecue marinades. Available in jars or cans. Once opened, should be refrigerated.

I K A N   B I L I S

Tiny anchovies about one inch in length that have been salted and dried. When shallow fried, they are very crispy and utterly delicious and more-ish. Rich in protein and full of vitamins and minerals, you can be pardoned for tucking in endlessly. Malays and Nonyas add a hot sambal sauce to it making it a dish in its own right. Try also recipe on page 81 where the delicate flavour of galanggal is balanced with tamarind, sugar and chillies, rendering this dish hot, sweet and sour.

Look out for ready gutted and beheaded ones as it saves time although when fried to a crisp you can eat them whole. However, most people are not too keen on the heads and the black gut which can be slightly bitter.

As a child I was always delegated this tedious task. Keep tightly lidded in a jar and refrigerate, well wrapped as they do have a fishy smell. Do not rinse before frying as they will lose their crispness.

K I A M C H Y E

Sometimes referred to as Kiamchye or pickled cabbage, these are mustard greens which are preserved in brine. Available fresh in vats in some Chinese supermarkets but more readily available in cans. Several varieties exist using different varieties of mustard greens. Drain brine and rinse in fresh water to remove excess salt. Keeps for a week refrigerated. Used in soups and stirfried with beansprouts or pork and fish. Similar to German sauerkraut but mustard greens retain their crunchiness.

L E M O N   G R A S S

This tall tropical grass resembling a spring onion has a subtle balmy lemon flavour and is a vital component in southeast Asian cuisine. However, it is the bulbous bottom half that is actually used because the top half is more woody and too fibrous. It is now available in many supermarkets in the fresh herb section. Used to flavour soups, it should be lightly crushed with a heavy object to release the oils. For making into curry pastes and rempah, cut off hard knob at the end, and slice very finely across the grain. You will see purplish rings in the middle. Continue slicing until you get to the bottom end which is greener and the stems are narrower.

Lemon grass can be kept in the refrigerator for weeks although it will dry out eventually. It can be frozen but as explained under galanggal, the juices will be lost when thawed and cause the bulb to be very fibrous, making slicing quite impossible, unless you mean to use it whole in soups.

L I L Y   B U D S

Also known as golden needles, these are the dried buds of yellow and orange day lilies. They are long 2-3in in length and golden brown in colour with a hard knob at one end where it is joined to the stem. Used in vegetarian dishes and favoured by Chinese Buddhist monks. They are mainly sold in Chinese supermarkets. Choose the ones that are fairly soft and not brittle so that you can tie them into a knot before soaking in water. This is because they will disintegrate in the cooking process and knotting them keeps them together. Also remove the hard stem at the end before soaking. They add texture to vegetarian dishes and have a mild garlic flavour. There is no substitute.

L I M E S

Apart from Kaffir lime there are two types of lime used in Southeast Asia. The larger variety (Limau Nipis) is more common in the west and is marginally smaller than the lemon with a thin green rind which sometimes changes to yellow. Its fragrance is more aromatic than lemons and it is easily available in the West.

The smaller tropical limes known as Limau Kesturi are the size of marbles and are less acidic. Ideal for making into lime juice as they are cheap and plentiful but less easily available in the West.

L I M E   L E A V E S

Come from a variety of lime called Kaffir Lime. The fruit of this lime tree has a dark green mottled appearance. The rind is used by the Thais to flavour curry pastes whilst the juice which is very aromatic but bitter, is used as a shampoo, believed to ward off evil spirits. The leaves too have a very strong aromatic flavour and are used in several dishes in Malay, Nonya and Indonesian cuisines. Sliced very finely, they are sprinkled over curry dishes and add a distinctive flavour. You normally find them floating in Thai Tom Yum soups.

Ensure the leaves are shiny and dark green when buying. Normally sold on the thick branch - beware of the thorns. The leaves can be frozen but they lose their bright green appearance when thawed out. They will dry out if left in the refrigerator for longer than 8-10 days. Tear the leaves to release the oils before cooking.

L O T U S   R O O T

A rhizome of the lotus plant, related to waterlilies, and used as a vegetable in China and Japan. It is beautifully porous and a dissection reveals a pretty pattern of air pockets. It should be peeled and dropped in salted water to stop it from discolouring. It can be added to soups, stirfried and deepfried as in tempura, or blanched and used as a salad. Also available in dried form or tinned in brine.

M I N T

The variety of mints available tends to depend on seasons as imports arrive from Thailand as well as the Middle Eastern countries. They are fairly interchangeable and any type of mint can be used in the dishes named in this book.

M U S T A R D   S E E D S

Used in both western and eastern cuisines, mustard seeds are readily available in spice jars in all supermarkets. In Indian cooking, they are liberally used to add a subtle flavour to vegetable dishes, lentils as well as curries, rice and fish dishes. I like the crunchy texture they add as well as the aesthetic appeal.

M U S T A R D   G R E E N S

Mustard greens (cabbage), are indigenous to both China and India and there are a few varieties, each with its own particular uses. Some are particularly good for pickles (Szechuan pickled cabbage)

O I L S

During my cookery classes I have often been asked what oil to use in cooking Southeast Asian food. Here are a few suggestions:

LARD. Freshly rendered pork or chicken fat is actually very fragrant and is today still preferred by the Chinese housewives and hawker chefs in Southeast Asia as a cooking medium. It is of course saturated fat and should be used with some restraint by the more health conscious. Commercially produced lard does not have the same quality and is best avoided.

GROUNDNUT (PEANUT) OIL burns at very high temperatures (around 260° C) and does not absorb odours and tastes as readily as vegetable oils. It is therefore more economical.

CORN OIL is made of polyunsaturated oil of maize and is fairly healthy to use. Can be expensive for deep frying but the fragrance is far superior to that of the cheaper blends.

BLENDED VEGETABLE OILS are fairly cheap to use and some brands are better than others so it is a case of experimentation. Fairly neutral in flavour and good for stirfrying.

SOYBEAN OIL is one of the cheapest oils on the market and used by manufacturers to blend with other oils. It has a slightly fishy taste.

SAFFLOWER OIL is purely unsaturated and, like soybean oil, has a slightly fishy taste.

SESAME OIL is extracted from sesame seeds and has a distinctive nutty flavour. Do not use sesame oil as a frying medium as it has a low burning point. Sesame oils are sold in pure form or blended with cheaper oils, the purer bottles being more expensive of course. Used as a marinade in many Chinese dishes and there is no reason why they could not be used as a basting oil if you like the flavour.

GHEE is clarified butter with milk solids removed. It has a higher burning temperature and is therefore a better frying medium than butter. The flavour of ghee is ideal for making rice pilaus, biryanis and curries but in these days of health consciousness, it should be used with restraint. Use vegetable ghee as an alternative.

The flavour of OLIVE OIL is too strong to be recommended for cooking Southeast Asian foods as it does not complement the ingredients used. However, it is used in Filipino cuisine because of its Spanish heritage.

O Y S T E R   S A U C E

Oyster sauce was originally made with just oysters, water and salt and thickened with cornflour. Caramel was later added to improve on the colour. These days however, manufacturers have added monosodium glutamate (MSG) to enhance the flavour and cheaper brands have capitalised on the qualities of MSG by reducing the amount of oysters. The rich flavour of oysters is ideal for seasoning plain steamed vegetables and many Cantonese restaurants douse everything in oyster sauce to cover up their inadequacies.

Should be refrigerated once opened. Vegetarian oyster sauce is now available.

P A L M   S U G A R

Also known as Gula Melaka, this comes from the sap of palms like coconut, palmyra and sugar palms and has a rich coconutty flavour used in many sweet recipes. It is normally sold in cylindrical blocks and sometimes wrapped in palm leaves. It should be dissolved in a little water and boiled to make into a syrup. It should then be strained as there are invariably foreign bodies. It goes particularly well with coconut based desserts. If a concentrate is required, the strained syrup can be boiled down to a thicker consistency.

Try serving it as ice cream topping, especially on coconut ice cream or in pancakes. Keeps indefinitely in a cool dry place.

R I C E   P A P E R

Made with watery rice gluten spread on round wooden trays to dry out into thin paper. Manufactured in Vietnam and Thailand although not used in any Thai recipes. Used as a spring roll wrapping. Make sure the contents are not damaged as they are so brittle and easily broken if dropped. Difficult to use if they are not perfectly formed.

S A F F R O N

A rare and expensive spice, saffron is the dried stigma of the small saffron crocus. Available in dried strands with variable quality depending on country of origin. Soak in tepid water to develop the colour and aroma and add towards the end of cooking as the flavour is lost through prolonged heat. Powdered saffron is more likely to be adulterated and of inferior quality. Used mainly in rice dishes such as risottos, paellas, pilaus and biryanis and complements seafood. Store in airtight container. Turmeric is often used as a substitute but add sparingly as turmeric has a much stronger flavour.

S A G O

Tiny white pearls made from sago palm starch. Used mainly in desserts throughout Southeast Asia. Available in packets. Soak before use to remove excess starch.

S E S A M E   S E E D S

Used as an important flavouring in Chinese cuisines. Toasted to a light brown, a delicious nutty flavour is released. Used in salad dressings and as a garnish. Pressed onto prawns on toast, they also add to the texture. Available loose in packets and fairly cheap.

SOYA SAUCES

This indispensable Chinese seasoning is a brown or light coloured salty liquid made from fermented soya beans. Dark soy has added molasses and is aged longer. It should therefore be used for the heartier dishes such as braised pork in dark soy (Red Cooked Pork). Light soy is more suitable for seafood, vegetables and marinades. For many years, British supermarkets stocked only the one strength of soy sauce which is neither dark or light but a combination of the two. However, the general public is now better informed and both light and dark soy sauces are available in supermarkets.

Mushroom soy is dark soy sauce flavoured with straw mushrooms and is richer in flavour. Use in place of dark soy if preferred. Thick soy is sweetened and concentrated soy for use in specific dishes. Good for adding to Char kuay teow, the Singaporean hawker dish of stirfried noodles which is cooked over a high heat and has a smoky flavour. Unlike other noodle dishes, this has to be very dry to achieve the required effect and thick soy fulfils that role as well as sweetening the dish.

Used also in Nonya Popiah which is unfried fresh spring roll. The treacle-like soy is drizzled over the pastry before the other ingredients are added and rolled up into spring rolls. Here again, ordinary soy sauce would be too 'runny' and would make the pastry soggy.

SPRING ROLL PASTRY

Frozen spring roll pastry are sold in squares in various sizes, 5 in, 8 in and 10 in. Will thaw within half an hour or so. Keep wrapped in damp cloth until ready to use as they will dry out very quickly and become too brittle. Unused pastry can be kept refrigerated in cling film or sealed food bags for a week to 10 days.

SZECHUAN PEPPER

A spice used only in Chinese cuisines. Reddish brown in colour and slightly larger than black peppercorns. Available in Chinese supermarkets and sold loose in plastic packets. Best stored in glass jar to preserve the flavour.

SZECHUAN PICKLED CABBAGE

These are preserved mustard green stems with added chilli and are therefore fairly pungent. Again, rinse before use to remove excess salt and chilli. Harder in texture and used mainly in soups where they need to be boiled for some while to tenderise.

TAMARIND

is extracted from the fleshy pulp surrounding the seeds contained in the largish pod of the tamarind tree. It has a sour but fruity taste and is therefore used as a souring agent in Indian seafood curries, lentil dishes and for chutneys and pickles. It is rich in vitamins and nutrients and believed to be good for curing liver and kidney complaints.

Sold in their pods but more commonly sold compressed into blocks. Pinch off a small section and soak in hot water to soften. When the mixture is cool enough to handle, work with fingers to remove the pulp from the seeds which are sometimes present. Thai brands are normally seedless and are therefore better value. Squeeze through fingers to strain the thick brown liquid over a sieve. A second extract of thinner consistency can also be obtained.
Tends to settle and separate and the watery solution can be skimmed off, leaving the concentrate below for spreading over prawns and fish as a marinade.

Indian supermarkets also stock tamarind concentrates in jars but the flavour is not as appealing.

TAUCEO

A fermentation of salted soya beans. Available also as crushed paste or bottled as whole beans in a brown saline suspension. When the latter are used, they should be strained and rinsed under running water to remove excess salt. Add a distinctive flavour to dishes but should be used with restraint as they are not necessarily to everyone's taste.

TEMPEH

Malays and Indonesians ferment whole soya beans which have been soaked and compressed into a cake with palm leaves. Served fried and cooked with fragrant and spicy sauces, they are delicious and have the crunchy texture of nuts. Will keep for weeks in a refrigerator or can be deep frozen. Available only in Filippino or Malaysian supermarkets.

TURMERIC

is another rhizome (underground stem) which is extensively used as a spice in powdered or fresh form. Indigenous to Southeast Asia this tropical perennial has found its way to India, China, Africa, the West Indies and Australia. The vivid orange yellow colouring of the root makes it easily identifiable. Used as one of the main spices in Indian curries, it is often called Indian Saffron. It has also medical applications and is recommended for skin diseases and to cure itching.

In Malaysia, Singapore and Indonesia, it is generally preferred in its fresh form as the flavour is obviously far superior to the powdered version. It also forms the bulk in making spice pastes and rempahs but as it tends to stain everything in contact, it is not always practical.

Turmeric leaves are sometimes used to flavour many Indonesian curries.

WANTUN PASTRY

is made of egg and wheatflour and readily available in Chinese supermarkets. Used for making pork and prawn wantuns. Will keep for a week or so in the refrigerator. If deep frozen, it thaws within half an hour or so. Keep well wrapped to stop it drying out or it will be too brittle to work with. Can be deep fried, steamed or added to soups. For the latter, boil separately in boiling water and strain to remove excess starch.

WATER CHESTNUTS

are an ancient Chinese swamp crop favoured for its succulent, crunchy and sweet white flesh. It can be enjoyed raw as a fruit or cooked in both sweet and savoury dishes. More importantly, the Chinese value its medicinal qualities as a tonic and its 'cooling' energies are prized as a delicious cure for overheated conditions.

Westerners are more likely to identify water chestnuts in its canned state but fresh water chestnuts in its black skins still caked with mud are now being imported and are available in good chinese supermarkets. Unpeeled they would remain fresh if kept in a well ventilated box for several weeks. They should be washed and peeled to reveal pure white flesh and soaked in water immediately to prevent discolouration. Boiling for 10 minutes in fresh water will help to preserve them once peeled.

WOOD EARS

Sometimes called Cloud ears, these mushrooms grow on rotting wood and are cultivated on oak trunks for commercial purposes. They have virtually no taste but are used for the most part for their resilient texture. However, the Chinese have always believed in their ability to reduce bloodclots and those about to have an operation, as well as pregnant mothers, are advised to refrain from consuming them. They are considered good for improving blood circulation.

In dried form, they resemble crumpled pieces of black paper but soaked in water they expand into translucent grey clouds with pretty frilly ears. Usually combined with lily flowers to enhance their medicinal effectiveness, they are often served in Buddhist vegetarian dishes.

Soak in hot water for about 15-20 minutes to soften. Check for sediments, bark particles and the hard stem where it has been attached to the tree. Keeps in its fried form indefinitely.

YAM BEANS

Called Bangkwang by the Nonyas and referrred to as Jicama in the Americas, yam bean is a tuber that looks like a spinning top. Light brown in colour, it could also pass as a turnip. It has a sweet and juicy flesh and is therefore just as delicious raw as cooked. It releases a lot of water when cooked. It appears in the Malaysian and Indonesian salad known as Rojak but is also used as a spring roll filling. A cheap vegetable in Southeast Asia but considerably more expensive when flown across to the West. It should keep for a week or so in the refrigerator but once the brown skin is peeled off to expose the crisp white flesh underneath it will deteriorate within a few days.

Yam beans are substantially starch with some fibre. They are low in vitamins but do contain some minerals and protein. Substitute water chestnuts if unavailable.

SAUCES

Light Soya sauce

Dark soya sauce

Fish Sauce

Sesame oil

Tauceo

POWDERED SPICES

Coriander

Turmeric

Cumin

Fennel

Fivespice

Chilli

DRIED AND TINNED INGREDIENTS

Coconut milk or powder

Candlenuts

Dried shrimps

Blachan

Gula Melaka

Metric and imperial measures, used throughout, are not strictly equivalent. Always use one, or the other, consistently throughout a recipe. Volume measurements are used where appropriate. One measuring cup contains 250ml (8oz); 1 teaspoon contains 5ml; 1 tablespoon contains 15ml or 3 teaspoons. Abbreviations are as follows: tablespoon (tbsp); dessertspoon (dsp); teaspoon (tsp).

Loon Fung Supermarket, 42 Gerrard Street, London W1. Tel: 0171 437 7179

See Woo Supermarket, 18-21 Lisle Street, London WC2. Tel: 0171 439 8325

Manila Market, 5 Hogarth Place, Earls Court, London SW10. Tel: 0171 373 8305

Phillipino Supermarket, 1 Kenway Road, Earls Court, London SW10. Tel: 0171 244 8562

Tawana Supermarket, 18 Chepstow Road, London W2. Tel: 0171 211 6316

Talad Thai Supermarket, 320 Upper Richmond Road, Putney, London SW18. Tel: 0181 789 8084

Sri Thai Supermarket, 56 Shepherds Bush Road, London W6. Tel: 0171 602 0621

Wang Thai Supermarket, 101-103 Kew Road, Richmond, Surrey. Tel: 0181 332 2959

Chuang Lee Trading, 98 Streatham High Road, London SW16 1BS. Tel: 0181 677 4033

Wing Yip Supermarket, 395 Edgware Road, Cricklewood, London NW2. Tel: 0181 450 0422

Wing Yip Supermarket, 373 Nechells Park Road, Nechells, Birmingham. Tel: 01327 6618

Wing Yip Supermarket, Oldham Road, Ancoats, Manchester M4 5HU. Tel: 0161 832 3215

Wing Yip Supermarket, 550 Purley Way, Croydon CR0 4RF. Tel: 0181 688 4880

Hoo Hing Supermarket, Hoo Hing House, Eastway Commercial Centre, Hackney, London E9 5NR. Tel: 0181 533 2811

Hoo Hing Supermarket, North Circular Road (A406), Park Royal, London NW10 5NR. Tel: 0181 838 3388

Hoo Hing Supermarket, Bond Road, Off Western Road, Mitcham, Surrey. Tel: 0181 687 2633

Asia Supermarket, 189 Ormeau Road, Belfast. Tel: 01232 326 396

China Supermarket, 32 Tudor Street, Cardiff, Wales. Tel: 01222 377 599

Hing Sing Chun Supermarket, 335 Leith Walk, Edinburgh. Tel: 0131 554 4333

Mata International Food, 51 Bold Street, Liverpool. Tel: 0151 709 3031

MENU IDEAS

COCKTAIL PARTY

Crudites with gado gado sauce
Siu mai
Crispy pork and prawn wantuns
Ngoh hiang
Popiah Goreng
Udang goreng
Beef and chicken Satay
Prawn wantuns
Larb

CELEBRATION DINNER

Wantun Prawns
Udang goreng
Ngoh hiang

Ayam Panggang
Rendang
Itek Chin
Ikan plachian
Chap chye
Nasi Ayam

DINNER PARTY

Popiah goreng
Larb

Opor Ayam
Teochew duck
Udang masak nanas
Babi pongtay
Sayur lodeh
Steamed rice

BUFFET LUNCH

Ayam Goreng
Sambal udang
Devilled Pork or chicken
Ikan Bilis tempra
Kalio
Gado gado
Char beehoon
Nasi goreng

FAMILY MEAL

Tunghoon soup

Ginger chicken
Ikan sental
Babi assam manis
Taugeh char kiamchye
Rice